God's Miracles

INSPIRATIONAL STORIES OF ENCOUNTERS WITH THE DIVINE

Lesley Sussman

ADAMS MEDIA CORPORATION
Avon, Massachusetts

*To my beautiful wife, Edita, who miraculously
found me when I was lost.*

Published by
Adams Media Corporation
57 Littlefield Street, Avon, MA 02322. U.S.A.
www.adamsmedia.com

ISBN: 1-58062-922-9

Printed in Canada.

J I H G F E D C B A

Library of Congress Cataloging-in-Publication Data
Sussman, Les.
God's miracles / Lesley Sussman.
p.   cm.
ISBN 1-58062-922-9
1. Miracles. I. Title.
BT97.3.S87 2003
231.7'3--dc21

2003002714

This publication is designed to provide accurate and authoritative information with regard to
the subject matter covered. It is sold with the understanding that the publisher is not engaged
in rendering legal, accounting, or other professional advice. If legal advice or other expert
assistance is required, the services of a competent professional person should be sought.
— From a *Declaration of Principles* jointly adopted by a Committee of the American Bar
Association and a Committee of Publishers and Associations

Many of the designations used by manufacturers and sellers to distinguish their prod-
ucts are claimed as trademarks. Where those designations appear in this book and
Adams Media was aware of a trademark claim, the designations have been printed with
initial capital letters.

While all the stories in this book are true, some of the names, dates, and places have
been changed to protect anonymity.

Cover photograph ©1998 Corbis Corp.

*This book is available at quantity discounts for bulk purchases.
For information, call 1-800-872-5627.*

Acknowledgments

The Spirit of God guided me through the writing of this book, and I would be remiss not to acknowledge the Creator first. I'd also like to thank my editors, Claire Gerus and Kate Epstein, and extend my deepest thanks to everyone in this book who shared their very personal miracle stories with me. Many thanks, as well, to Carolyn Collie at the *Christian Science Journal* for her help on this project as well as others, Father Charles Crespo for his prayers, and one special person who always inspires me—Rabbi Joseph H. Gelberman. Last but not least, thanks to Marshall Klein, an agent extraordinaire and a pretty good human being.

Foreword

Years ago when I was a young journalism student, my instructors would always try to instill in me the importance of being "objective" when covering a news story. Over the years, as a newspaper reporter, I did my best to obey that edict—not always successfully.

I'm proud to say that in researching and writing this book I again violated the edict that calls for objectivity. In fact, I found it literally impossible not to become deeply and personally involved with each and every moving account of God's miracles that complete strangers related to me. Not only was I often moved to tears by these stories, I was also deeply honored and grateful that so many people would share such personal parts of their lives with me.

All my life I've been searching for miracles, so it was with a sense of awe—and a touch of envy—that I listened to these amazing testimonies of God's miraculous intervention in people's lives. Often, I went to sleep with snatches of interviews still playing through my mind. No, objectivity was certainly impossible in the writing of this book.

What I most enjoyed in doing the research was learning—not for the first time—that miracles are not just a once-in-a-while phenomenon. I was quite amazed at the large number of people out there who have experienced such extraordinary events in their lives.

In fact, if you go on the Internet, you will find hundreds of testimonies about miraculous healings, recoveries, rescues, and other supernatural events. Miracles, it seems, are happening to an awful lot of people much of the time—and we should all be grateful for that. Don't let the skeptics tell you otherwise.

I'm not exactly a newcomer to the subject of miracles. Over the years I have written a couple of books on the subject. But this particular book is quite special to me because I was struggling through my own health crisis during its writing. Listening to and writing these true accounts gave me strength and inspiration. It also helped to reinforce my faith, which sometimes goes on vacation. I certainly hope upon reading these true and remarkable stories that you experience the same inspiring feelings.

Sitting on the top of my computer console is a paperweight that I recently purchased in one of those ninety-nine-cent discount stores that can be found throughout New York City. This inexpensive paperweight consists of a glass bird perched upon a stone. What is special to me about the stone is that the word "Believe," is carved on it. Under that carving with a pen I added: Believe that:

You are healthy ~ You are prosperous ~
You are blessed ~ You are healed ~ You are lucky

Turning my eyes from my computer during the writing of the book, this paperweight was the first thing that would catch my attention. It constantly reminded me how important it is to believe in God—and in yourself— as a team or a partnership. It is a theme that the ancient Jewish mystics used to emphasize, and such a belief in this spiritual alliance goes a long way toward making miracles happen.

In writing this book, I tried to include a variety of miracle stories. I discovered numerous dramatic healing accounts, and have included many of them in the pages ahead. But I also wanted to document more than just the kinds of incredible miracle stories that often make the cover of *Oprah Magazine*.

I fully agreed with the Rev. Paul Crampton, director of Chaplaincy Services at the White Memorial Medical Center in Los Angeles, who said in his interview that sometimes the most impressive miracles are the more subtle ones—such as those having to do with love and forgiveness.

I also tried to include accounts of miracles from all the major faiths to show that God has no favorite religion. All He asks is that you turn to Him in your time of need (although staying in close touch would be nice all the time). But I was not successful in finding miracle stories from all the great faiths, despite my best efforts. I could not, for example, get anyone who practiced Islam or

Buddhism to share a miracle account with me. I hope I can correct this in the next book.

In doing the interviews, there was one question I asked almost everyone with whom I spoke, and that had to do with whether or not they grew up in a religious household and with a belief in miracles. What I learned is that God works wonders in our lives whether or not we grew up religiously, and that not hearing about miracles as a youngster didn't stop anyone from experiencing them.

One of my all-time favorite television programs is *The X-Files*. The show always concludes with this message flashed on the screen: "The Truth Is Out There." I couldn't agree more. I believe that Truth is called God and I know that this Holy Spirit is out there and waiting for us to find Him. All it takes is faith, trust, and prayer.

If you are ill, fearful, anxious, alone, or hurting in any way, I hope that by reading this book you will be filled with the Spirit of God and begin your transformation to a healthy and prosperous life. It can happen in an instant. If, on the other hand, you are in good health, may this book fill you with the confidence and awareness that God is and will always continue to be by your side.

Shalom, my friends, shalom.

Lesley Sussman
New York City
January 2003

It was the winter of 1999 and Linda Ferris, a nurse, was busy working at the Henry Ford Medical Clinic in Detroit when her phone rang. "I said hello several times, and I heard a familiar silence," she recalls. "It was the kind of silence I always got when Mom was too choked up to tell me some bad news—like when one of the grandchildren was sick."

When her mother, Dolores Milen, finally broke the silence, the news wasn't about one of the kids, but about herself. "The doctor called and I need to repeat my mammogram," Linda's mother said. "He found two suspicious masses."

Linda became numb at those words. Then her professional response kicked in. "I talked to my mother about it like I've done so many times with patients and tried to keep from showing that I was upset."

When she hung up the phone, Linda swung into action, scheduling a follow-up mammogram for the next week. She went over to her mother's house to reassure her, but she still felt numb.

The first thing she did when she got home was to pray that her mother would be all right. Over the next couple of days, waiting for the results of the second mammogram, she began asking everyone she knew to pray, too.

Linda had been raised moderately religious, and had attended both the Baptist and Presbyterian churches as a child. She had always been interested in religion, and had attended church with her brother even when her parents didn't go. But Linda had come to believe in the power of prayer through her work as a nurse. She had seen the power of a strong prayer life and will to live. Faith and prayer had mitigated her own experience of chronic fatigue syndrome.

Her mother had always been strong—Dolores had raised five children and several grandchildren, and nursed Linda's father after a stroke. Linda knew—hoped—that she would be all right.

But Linda's worries were not over yet. The second mammogram showed two well-defined masses, suspicious for breast cancer. Her mother would need a biopsy as soon as possible.

Linda was stunned as she tried to comfort the mother who had always been her rock, through her childhood and her own recent divorce.

When she got home the night after the results of the second mammogram had come, Linda was emotionally exhausted. "I lay on the couch in total darkness and just cried and prayed to God. The next day I couldn't do anything. I felt as if I were paralyzed."

Linda forced herself to go to work, although she found it very difficult to concentrate or talk to patients with the confidence she once had. All the while, she was worrying about her mother. Through her professional connections, Linda got her mother the next available appointment at the Karmanos Cancer Centre in Detroit in two weeks. "The longest two weeks of our lives," says Linda.

Linda filled the time asking everyone she came into contact with to pray for Dolores, as well as their pastor, her friends, and her brothers and sisters. Every day she went over to Dolores's house just to be near her.

The morning finally came for Linda to drive her mother down to the Karmanos Cancer Centre for the biopsy. The feeling that engulfed her that morning surprised her. "Somehow, I felt strong, with a confidence that I know I couldn't have gotten all on my own, but from a Higher Power," she proclaims. "I knew there were hundreds of people praying for my mother and I just had faith that God would hear those prayers and perform a miracle. And so all the way to the Centre I just held on to this feeling."

But Linda's resolve broke when her mother disappeared into the examining room, and she burst into tears. "I wanted so much to be with her, to hold her hand like she'd done for me so many times in my life. She was the most dedicated and loyal mother and wife. I could always go to her with a problem and we could talk about anything."

Linda began to pray in the waiting room. When she looked up, she was surprised to see her mother standing before her, crying. "They didn't do it," she announced.

"What? What do you mean they didn't do it?" said the incredulous daughter.

Dolores smiled and took a seat next to her daughter. The ultrasound hadn't shown anything. The doctors had several films from the prior mammograms to compare, and they called in other doctors to confirm it. The masses were simply gone. "Lady, we can't biopsy something that's not there," one of the doctors had said.

Linda stared at her mother. All she could do was mutter to herself, "They couldn't find it—it's completely gone."

The next moments were absolutely magical, Linda says. "We walked back to the elevator, rode down to the lobby, and as we began to realize what they had just said, we wrapped our arms around each other. We just stood there holding on for dear life. I didn't realize the lobby was full of people sitting in chairs all around us when I blurted out, 'Mom, God healed you.' Suddenly I noticed tears of joy on my mother's face as people all around us were smiling."

All the way home the two women cried, and laughed, and cried again.

It has been more than a year since that miraculous event, and Linda says it seems as if it only happened yesterday.

Linda's mother continued to go for mammograms every six months. The results never changed. "I will always thank God for the miraculous gift He gave us."

*D*enver Nuggets play-by-play radio announcer Jerry Schemmel will never forget July 19, 1989, when he and his best friend, Jay Ramsdell, boarded United Airlines Flight 232 from Denver to Chicago.

The men were the last two passengers to board the crowded plane, and they had to sit apart. Like many other passengers, they had been scheduled to fly earlier on a flight that had been canceled because of mechanical difficulties.

Takeoff and the first hour of the flight passed without

anything unusual happening. Then, just about fifteen minutes from the Sioux City airport, the plane suddenly began to shake and the passengers heard a tremendous explosion. One of the engines had exploded and completely crippled the plane's hydraulic system.

Jerry later learned that the damage to the plane was so severe, the pilot was not sure he could keep the aircraft aloft until it could reach the airport. But he kept the plane in the air by skillfully balancing the remaining engines.

The passengers began to pray. Then the plane crash-landed at the airport with a terrifying jolt.

Jerry can still hear the sickening sound of crunching metal as the plane started to flip over. He and the other passengers were violently rocked and tossed in their seats. There were bumping noises and the screech of metal as the bottom of the plane dragged along the runway and broke up into sections.

Rows 22 to about 30—the section Jerry was seated in—flipped over once and slid along the runway upside down. Then it slid off the right side of the runway into a cornfield. Jerry was hanging upside down and still strapped to his seat. The man next to him was dead. The woman across the aisle from him was missing. The flight attendant who'd been in the jump seat facing him was gone.

When the plane finally skidded to a halt, Jerry thanked God for sparing his life. He unbuckled his safety belt and tumbled down to the ceiling of the upside-down plane. He could see no way out.

The compartment was beginning to fill up with thick dark smoke. Jerry was sure the miracle of his surviving the crash would be for naught. He would burn or suffocate.

But suddenly he spotted some sunlight pouring through an opening in the twisted metal where the front section of the plane had been. He thanked God again, knowing that escape was possible.

Jerry was suffering from an injured back, a sprained ankle, smoke inhalation, and serious abrasions, but he and several other survivors helped dazed passengers to their feet and pushed them out of the plane. Jerry's best friend was dead.

Finally, the smoke grew so thick, Jerry was forced to leave the plane. He couldn't see or breathe.

Now standing outside the plane, Jerry was about to run from the twisted and burning plane wreckage, fearing it would explode. "In the movies and on TV, every time you get outside of something, it explodes, and that's what I was thinking about," he relates.

But suddenly Jerry heard a baby crying from somewhere inside the wreckage. "I said, 'Oh, my God, I've got to save that child.' I wasn't trying to be a hero. It was just something that came over me. It was an instinctive thing and I just didn't think about it."

Was it something other than instinct that propelled him into action? Jerry has often wondered whether God spoke to him at that moment. He crawled back into the wreckage on all fours. He could hardly see and he was choking. The only thing he knew to do was follow the sounds of the child's sobs.

He found her somewhere toward the middle of the wrecked airplane. She was partially buried in debris. She had been sitting on the floor between her mother's feet in row 11, and had been thrown almost twenty rows. But her only injury was a cut under her eye.

Cradling the infant in his arms and choking from the fumes, Jerry slowly crawled out of the plane.

When he emerged, the girl's parents were standing on the tarmac. "They looked at me like I was an angel or something," says Jerry. Both parents told him later they thought their child was dead.

There were 184 survivors that day. And one special miracle child among them.

With only $15 left until payday, Robert Melton of Plainview, Texas, was not sure how he and his wife, Kimberly, were going to manage. And he had promised her that they would go out to eat after Sunday church services. But he resolved that he would let her enjoy a Sunday meal while he fasted.

The thirty-four-year-old native Californian, who was raised in Texas, recalls that his family always took church seriously. "Both my folks belonged to the Four Square Church and I grew up hearing all kinds of stories about miracles," he offers. "But it wasn't until nineteen ninety-two that I experienced one of my own."

Robert had just started working at a meat-packing company and was not making much money. He always tithed to the church, too, and that was more money out of his small paycheck.

Going to church that Sunday morning, Robert recalls that his financial situation had him feeling down. All of the money he had until payday was in cash in his pocket. Attending church service that morning with Robert and his wife was Robert's father-in-law, Paul Cunningham, a noted evangelist, who would join Robert and Kimberly for lunch. It pained Robert not to be able to afford to pick up his tab. During the service, Robert offered up some private prayers asking God for financial help.

Kimberly, Robert, and Paul decided on a nearby restaurant. The wind was blowing thirty to forty miles per hour that day and the car was shaking as Robert parked it. He was shocked to see some money lying on the grass, in spite of the wind.

When he walked over, Robert saw that it was a $20 bill. "Great, I can eat today," thought Robert. He went back to the car to open the door for Kim and right there by the back wheel was another $20 bill, oddly motionless in the wind.

Robert says he had no doubt that this was a miracle—

an answer to his prayers in church that morning. "I had paid my tithes to the church even when I couldn't afford it, because the Bible encourages you to always give back something of what you earn. Even if I were making ten dollars a week, I would tithe. And now I was being rewarded. I just knew that God had provided for me that day."

If Robert thought that miracles happen just once in a lifetime, he was wrong. A few months later—still short on money—he and his family had driven to Shawnee, Oklahoma, for a tent revival. They had driven six hours to get there, and had to spend one night in a motel, eating out throughout the trip.

"Remember the forty-dollar miracle in Plainview?" Paul asked him over dinner one evening, when Robert expressed his concerns about the expense of the trip and the financial pressures he was under. Paul reminded Robert that God had not gone out of the miracle business.

Robert remembers leaving the restaurant at about 1 A.M. As he was about to get into his car he looked down at his feet—he has no idea why—and he saw a bill, rolled up like a straw. Bending, he said to Kimberly, "Oh, look, someone dropped a dollar." But as Robert stood, and unrolled the bill, he was amazed—he was holding a $100 bill. His first thought was "God is truly a miracle worker!"

Robert was able to pay off some pressing bills with the money, but his finances were still troubling him. Some weeks later, on yet another windy West Texas day with the wind blowing at least thirty miles per hour, Robert decided to do some grocery shopping. He parked his car and got out, and up there against the right rear passenger door tire was another $20 bill, seemingly impervious to the wind.

Robert says he often shares this testimony in church and at revival meetings. "There's more than coincidence to what happened to me," he declares. "Everywhere I go I get up and tell people about this financial miracle. It wasn't a lot of money, but I am more than grateful for what was given me."

Robert is now doing much better financially than in years past. "God got me out of the hole when I most needed Him," he proclaims. "I'm certain it had to do with my tithing. I tell everyone who is struggling finan-cially to tithe first and then pray, and God will provide them with what they need."

*I*t was about 9 P.M. and Marshall Dudley was tired. He and his wife were driving through Knoxville, Tennessee. The two-lane road was narrow and poorly lit.

Donna saw the dark shape in front of them first, the size of a truck. Marshall was driving about fifty miles an hour. The truck was completely dark because it was very dirty—Marshall could hardly see it. And there were no lights on the back of it.

Donna was so scared that she started making some noises and pointing frantically, but she couldn't get any sound out of her mouth. Marshall was afraid Donna was having a heart attack.

When Marshall looked, he was almost right up on this truck—maybe not more than twenty feet away.

The truck had completely blocked his side of the road. There was a ditch to the right, but no time to drive into it. "All I could think of was that if I swung my car left, the right side of the car where my wife was sitting would hit the truck. If I swung right, my side of the car would hit the truck. I just knew that no matter what I did, one of us was going to die."

In that instant, Marshall chose to hit the truck with his side of the car, expecting it would kill him but that his wife might survive. He swung the wheel as far as he could to the right. A split second later, he had both hands on the steering wheel going straight down the road. They were about 500 feet in front of the truck. He could see its headlights receding in his rearview mirror.

Donna recovered her powers of speech for the first time since she spotted the truck. "What happened? How did you do that? How did we end up in front of the truck? I thought we were dead!"

Marshall wasn't sure, at first, that he had done any-thing—he thought he and Donna were dead, on the spirit side of life in what he describes as "some kind of dream stage." He says, "I also worried that any minute now my wife was going to realize that we were dead and she was going to be real mad at me."

All he could say for a while was "I just don't want to talk about it." An electrical engineer, Marshall considers himself scientifically minded. Although he believes in God, he had never thought much about miracles.

Marshall says that over the years he has given much thought to what happened that night, and the only plausible explanation he can come up with is that he and his wife experienced a bona fide miracle. "It's the best category that I can think of," he asserts. "My wife certainly believes it's a miracle and she credits God for it." He laughs. "I think that between the two of us, one of us has a good friend in high places."

*J*oseph Sobel was nineteen on that hot summer day in 1943 when he had taken his future wife, Jenny, out in a rowboat in New York City's Central Park. In an effort to impress her, he began horsing around. Jenny told him to sit down. "But since when does a know-it-all teenager listen to a pretty young woman he's trying to impress?" says Joseph now. Soon enough, the boat capsized.

It might have been funny—even refreshing—except that Joseph had never learned how to swim. He had been raised in Poland, and it had never come up.

"We learned how to run from the anti-Semites, but not swim," he laughs now. Jenny, who knew how to swim a little, made it back to the dock. Joseph finally managed to grab onto the side of the boat, and one of the lifeguards swam out and got him safely to shore.

Although raised in an Orthodox Jewish household, where his father, a rabbi, often spun Sabbath stories about miracles, Joseph didn't view his near-drowning accident as anything miraculous. He says the only thing he got out of that experience was the knowledge that he and water just didn't mix.

But there was another hot summer day and another near escape. This time Joseph was at the beach on Coney Island. Everyone else seemed to be at Coney Island, too, and the area near the shore was choked with people. He had taken a few swimming lessons, and he felt confident enough to walk into the water just up to his chest, even though it would take him past the rope swimmers were supposed to stay behind. It was Friday afternoon and Joseph had to be back for the start of the Sabbath, so all he had time for was a quick dip.

From out of nowhere a huge wave appeared. It knocked Joseph completely off his feet. His swimming lessons were no help to him now, but as he flailed, a lifeguard rescued him. No harm had been done.

Joseph laughs at the memory. "I'd read Bible stories

of Moses parting the water—I even read somewhere that Jesus walked on water. But one thing for sure—the waters never parted for me and I was never able to walk on it. For some reason water was always trying to pull me underneath."

The third time he nearly drowned Joseph does believe a miracle took place. He was about thirty—recently married to the woman he had almost drowned in Central Park. He had gone to the free neighborhood Olympic-size pool in a park just two blocks from his apartment in Manhattan.

Joseph put on his bathing suit and told Jenny he was going for a quick swim. "The look she gave me should've been a warning," he recalls. "Her eyes said, 'Joseph, you know that you and water are not a good mix.'"

But just as he didn't sit down in the rowboat in Central Park when she told him to, Joseph didn't pay Jenny any attention. He went straight for the ten-foot section of the pool, which was deserted except for a couple of teenagers who were absorbed in showing off for each other. Joseph was a confident swimmer, now—until he developed a cramp in his leg.

He couldn't kick and he panicked. He was coughing, going under and coming up, and everybody was too busy to even notice—they probably thought he was horsing around. Even the lifeguard was busy talking to a pretty young woman. He tried to shout, but his mouth was filled with water.

Suddenly he sensed a man swimming next to him, someone far too large to be one of the teenagers. He couldn't see the man because the sun seemed to catch his eye every time he came up.

The man was swimming beside him and supporting him, like a professional lifeguard would do. A calm came over Joseph. "I felt like I was in God's hands," he says.

When he reached the side of the pool, Joseph wanted to get a good look at his rescuer. But there was no one there.

Joseph is eighty-three and now lives on Brighton Beach, with a view of the Atlantic. He has never again considered the possibility that he and water "don't mix." "That miracle in the swimming pool was enough to convince me that I'm protected. I just know that God stretched out His hand to save me."

*J*oy Maybe has always believed in miracles. She was raised as an Episcopalian in the Deep South by devout parents who were very religious and active in the church, and family prayer was a part of their lives. Miracle stories from the Bible were regular topics of dinner conversation, and her father and grandmother especially liked to tell these stories.

Joy has retained the practice of praying every morning when she awakens. She asks God to guide her words, her thoughts, and her actions as she goes about her daily activities. And just before she goes to sleep, she thanks Him for another day.

So it's natural that prayer and faith are a part of the way she approaches her job as a nurse. Joy entered nursing school in Baltimore, Maryland, at the age of seventeen, and upon graduation moved to New York City. She worked as a nurse for four years at Mount Sinai Hospital, after which she accepted employment working in the private office of a cancer specialist. Throughout those years, Joy says she witnessed some remarkable recoveries by critically ill patients who responded to prayer after doctors had given up all hope.

"I always prayed over my patients and I saw a lot of things," she attests. "I specifically remember one private patient of mine—he and his family were also my very good friends—who got meningitis. We took him to the hospital where he was treated for several months.

"One day the doctor told me, 'Joy, I've done everything I can do for this patient; it's up to you now.'" She laughs. "He knew that I was a very religious person. In fact, some of the doctors used to kid me that I had 'a hotline to God.' He said, 'Do whatever you think will help because I can't help him any further.'"

Joy and a friend made arrangements to take the seriously ill patient to Pittsburgh to attend a faith-healing session with a prominent healer. This healer had cured the son of one of her friends of cancer.

The patient went into a coma a few days before the scheduled trip, so Joy and her friend went on to Pittsburgh without him and attended the faith healing service early the next morning. "If you've never seen a faith healing service, nobody can describe it to you," says Joy.

"Even before the doors opened at seven o'clock there were people already congregating there," she relates. "They were singing praise songs in five different languages. There were people there on stretchers and in wheelchairs. There was a doctor who was acting as an usher. His daughter had been cured of cancer by this healer."

Throughout the service, Joy prayed for her friend's recovery. She was surprised when an usher tapped her on the shoulder and asked her to come up to the stage.

She got up to the pulpit, and the healer put her hand over her. Suddenly, she could see someone in a white gown—like an angel. "It was such a strange feeling—a kind of certainty that everything was all right."

Joy remembers glancing at the clock as she was led back to her seat. It was 1 P.M. She fell down on her knees to pray. She heard the healer tell the audience, "Someone has just been to the pulpit who is not praying for herself. She is praying for a very dear friend."

Joy was amazed. She hadn't spoken to anyone about her friend in the coma. She heard the healer speaking again, "God is right now curing her friend. He is going to be all right." The feeling that all would be well came over Joy again.

When Joy and her friend returned to their hotel room, she immediately called her friend's room at the hospital. She could hear the man who had so recently been in a coma talking in the background. The coma had lifted at just about 1 P.M.—exactly the same time that the faith healer said he would be healed.

~

But the miraculous healing of Joy's own illness would take her farther and amaze her still more. In the late l990s, Joy was diagnosed with a skin disease known as shingles, an infection caused by the same virus that causes chicken pox. The itchy, painful condition wasn't responding to medication, and her doctor said there was nothing else he could do for her.

A short while later Joy received a call from her friend Paula, who was a practicing psychic. Paula told Joy about a Buddhist group in Queens that was responsible for some amazing healings.

As an Episcopalian from the Deep South, Joy didn't know anything about Buddhism, but she told Paula she'd do anything that could make her feel better.

It was a Monday when Paula and Joy went to the Buddhist temple. An elderly Japanese woman greeted them and brought Joy into an interior room where she was asked to lie down on a straw mat. "I had no idea what was going on," she relates. "I could hear chanting and prayers in Japanese, and before I knew it I had fallen asleep. When we left, this elderly woman asked me to come back. So I made an appointment for the following Friday."

When she returned home, there was no noticeable change in her condition, but she went back to the temple on Friday. The same elderly woman greeted her and Paula, and the ritual of chants and prayers was repeated.

Joy took off her clothes in front of the mirror that night and was amazed to see her skin restored. All of the redness and flaking was gone.

Joy scheduled a visit to her physician. After examining her, he said, "I don't know what you've done, but there's nothing there." She laughs at that memory. "He knows that I'm always exploring and when I told him what had happened, he agreed it was a miracle."

Although Joy had known that miracles could heal her patients, she was amazed at her own recovery, and especially at its speed. "I believed a lot in prayer—but I certainly didn't think that things would happen that fast. I've seen things happen to my patients when I've prayed for them—I've seen conditions disappear—but I didn't expect it to happen that way to me."

The fact that Buddhist prayer was the agent of her healing doesn't surprise Joy at all, even though the religion was so exotic to her. Her father had always taught her that no religious teaching is bad. "The only time a religious teaching is bad is when people twist that teaching to fit their own selfish needs.

"There's only one God, so why shouldn't I have been healed through the Buddhist religious tradition? I walked into that temple with an open mind and I received a miracle healing from God—but from a different culture. This was no coincidence. It was simply God listening and answering prayers as He does to people from all faiths and cultures."

$\mathcal{S}$andi Dalton was a young critical care nurse working in the surgical intensive care unit at Swedish Hospital in Seattle. In the summer of 1977, she had a patient who had just undergone open-heart surgery.

The waiting room was filled to capacity with this patient's loved ones, praying unceasingly. The woman's husband of thirty-six years was completely devoted. His lifelong love for his wife was obvious when he visited her for the first time following the surgery. The tubes and wires that were attached to her could not distract him or frighten him. His eyes went immediately to her face, his hand to her hand.

At first the woman's recovery from the surgery progressed normally. Her vital signs were stable and she responded appropriately to immediate postoperative treatment. But her cognitive response had not returned. Sandi became nervous when, after twenty-four hours, the patient showed no signs of waking.

The patient began to show signs and symptoms of a deteriorating neurological status. Patients undergoing heart surgery are at risk of suffering strokes during the procedure, and Sandi feared the woman had had a massive stroke. By the third day, symptoms of deterioration were pronounced. All the experts had been consulted. The doctors had run out of medical options.

Sandi always finds it dreadful to recognize when there is nothing more that medicine can do. "It's like trying to hold water in my cupped hands," she says. "No matter how hard I try, the water continues to leak through my fingers until there's nothing left."

The medical staff tried to help the woman's family say goodbye. As days passed, fewer and fewer friends and family came. Each in his or her own time, in his or her own way, was able to release her to God.

But the woman's husband never gave up. Day after

day, night after night, he prayed in that waiting room. Sandi felt almost frustrated at his inability to accept the inevitable. At the time, she had a rather lukewarm attitude toward religion.

Two weeks had passed since the woman's surgery and her condition was still critical. She had never awakened. "It was about nine-thirty on a Saturday morning, and the surgeon and I were standing by her bedside discussing her care," Sandi relates. "We weren't even looking at the patient or paying any attention to her because we figured she wasn't even cognizant."

Right in the middle of a sentence Sandi heard a throat being cleared. She looked down, and the woman's eyes were open. The patient smiled and said: "Hi."

Sandi says she "floated" down the hallway to the waiting room. She rushed over to the woman's husband and said: "Your wife would like to speak to you." The man's response astonished her. "He didn't even look surprised. The look on his face was just one of relief. He had never doubted for one moment that God would return his wife to him. His only question was when.

"We walked back to the unit and I watched through my tears as he bent down and gently kissed her. They then wrapped their arms around each other." Sandi looked up and saw the heart surgeon, a staunch egotist who had never believed that a husband's faith could affect anything where medical science could not, jumping up and down at her bedside, laughing and clapping his hands like a delighted child.

yan Roberts had an unusual dream on the morning of August 18, 1999.

He was lying on his back in a forest. He knew something really awful had just happened and that he had to stay very still. There were people gathered around him and Ryan asked them to pray with him, which they did. He saw a photographer, taking pictures. Then he looked up and saw the bottom of a helicopter. He was being suspended from it with a fifty-foot rope, and he thought to himself, "Gosh, this is my first helicopter ride and I don't even get to enjoy it."

Next Ryan saw himself riding in an ambulance, then in the emergency ward of a hospital. He was flat on his back, slowly backing into a creamy white tube with a red light whizzing around his head. Then someone was showing him an x-ray with strange markings.

Next, he heard a voice saying, "All these things must come to pass, but I will be with you through it all. There will be the right people in the right place at the right time." Ryan was certain it was the voice of God, who also said, "You will fully recover."

Ryan, who was twenty-one and a student, decided not to tell his parents about the dream, although it disturbed him. After all, it was only a dream.

But on September 5, Ryan and two friends went mountain biking on Powderface Trail in the foothills west of Calgary, Alberta, Canada.

The three young men set out at about 1:30 P.M. It was a perfect day for mountain biking with the sun occasionally poking through the clouds. They knew it would be the last mountain bike ride of the season before the snow flew.

Going up the trail was no problem for the bicyclists. Ryan describes himself as a moderately good rider. He was a confident sports player. In fact, prior to his spiritual awakening, Ryan describes that sports, including

bicycling and basketball, were among his gods. He had
extensive experience bicycling on the type of terrain he
was coping with that day.

But on the descent it happened.

Ryan saw a rock sticking up in the middle of the
path, and he veered right. His tire must have hit another
rock, because the next thing he knew, he was skidding
off the pathway and over the hill.

Ryan struggled to maintain control of the bike, but it
only made matters worse. The last thing Ryan can
remember was tumbling down the forty-five-degree
incline, and then he blacked out. One of his friends
recalls that he tried to disentangle himself from the bike,
but that it hit something in the woods, sending him cata-
pulting back-first over a thirty-foot cliff.

Ryan's friends watched the accident as if it were in
slow motion. They ran down to find him at the bottom of
a gully, about fifty feet down.

Ryan's scraped-up goggles had snapped in half, protecting his eyes from damage, but the rest of his body
took a severe beating. An excruciating pain seemed to
come from his neck and to radiate throughout his body.

Holding his neck as straight as he could with both
hands, Ryan walked out to the pathway. Just then a
hiker appeared who turned out to be a registered nurse.
She told Ryan to lie down and keep his neck as still as

possible. There was Ryan, just as his dream had foretold, lying flat on his back in the forest.

About five minutes later the hiker's three friends joined the group—a doctor and two other nurses.

There will be the right people in the right place at the right time, the voice in the dream had said. "I had just tumbled off a thirty-foot cliff and here I'm surrounded by four medical personnel just as the Lord had told me."

Lying on the ground, Ryan tried to tell everyone around him about his dream and how in the dream he and all the people standing around him had prayed for his recovery. To his amazement, everyone joined hands and began to pray.

By now, more people had gathered. Although some had cell phones, none of them worked, because of the elevation. But, amazingly, a park ranger responding to another accident came by with an emergency medical phone and summoned help. Ryan was placed on an immobilization board, and was second in line to be air-lifted out of the area.

Ryan waited four hours for a rescue helicopter, drifting in and out of consciousness.

When the helicopter finally came, Ryan's head was strapped down tight to the immobilization board. All he could see was air, and a 100-foot rope dangling. *It's happening, again*, he thought. *The dream is happening, again.*

And he blacked out. Unbeknownst to him, a news photographer had come to the scene to photograph his dramatic airlift, fulfilling another one of the dream's predictions.

The rescue workers reported that he kept repeating five words: "It's okay. I'll be all right." Whenever he came to consciousness, Ryan remembers recalling God's words of reassurance to him in his dream.

"God had told me I would survive this, so I knew that I would be all right—without a doubt," he declares. "He didn't leave any doubt in my mind as to the events that were taking place, and what was to come. When God blessed me with that dream, He was shining a floodlight on what was going to happen in my life."

Ryan speculates that God might have caused this accident to happen for a reason. "I think I needed a slap in the face to genuinely appreciate Him and life. I also think God had a plan to use me as an example to inspire others.

"Not only did I grow in my understanding of the Almighty, but people around me grew in their faith by leaps and bounds when they saw how the Lord had worked in me and through me. None of this spiritual growth for myself or others would have happened unless the accident took place."

After Ryan arrived at the hospital, the doctors

immediately ordered a CAT scan, MRIs, and x-rays. He opened his eyes for about two seconds as he was going into the creamy white-colored CAT scan machine, and he saw a red light rotating around his head.

When Ryan regained consciousness in the emergency room at about 9 P.M., he had a sense of overwhelming peace.

Neither the x-ray showing that the C2 vertebrae in his neck had broken in half, nor the fact that he needed surgery, could shake his sense of peace and his confidence that he would recover. The doctors said he could be quadriplegic for life, if he didn't die first. It's rare to survive this kind of fracture, called a "hangman's fracture."

The surgery was scheduled for the following Saturday. His family and friends held a prayer session asking God for his blessings. Ryan asked the doctors and nurses to pray with him before the surgery, which they did, contributing to his sense of calm and well-being.

The next thing that Ryan recalls is awakening with a wretched taste of anesthetics in his mouth. Groggily, he asked the nurse how the operation went. "The doctor said it was ninety-nine percent perfect," she told him.

Ryan was in the hospital for a little over a week. "Never was God's love clearer to me than during that challenging time when I looked out my hospital room window one clear fall night. I gazed at the pastel pink sunset sky, the foothills in the foreground, and snow-capped glistening mountain peaks as the backdrop. And for just a fleeting moment I understood that His plan was not only for my life, but for all humanity.

"I understood then how massive and awesome God truly is and how precious our time here really is. I'm not completely sure why it took such a slap in the face for me to genuinely appreciate life, but I do know that there have been so many blessings that have come from this incident, I can't even begin to count them."

Ryan's recovery was speedy. One day after his surgery he was on his feet walking. Nine days later, he walked out of the hospital and back home, his head supported by a brace-like device called a Halo vest. His recovery took about four months, and eight months later he was playing basketball again.

Ryan says as a youngster he was always fascinated by the miracle stories he heard talked about in church. "But I always thought miracles were something that happened a long time ago—that it was something God didn't do today," he exclaims. "Now, of course, I know differently.

"I know for certain that God is always right by my side," he declares.

*R*ev. Rick Cooper, a pastor in Minor, Alabama, didn't think much about the weather report he heard that Wednesday morning about disturbances in Mississippi and Louisiana, even though severe weather in Minor, a suburb of Birmingham, usually originated from these two states. There are so many tornadoes and tornado warnings in that area of the South that, he says, "after a while you just ignore it." He had served as a pastor in Minor for nearly two decades. It was the Wednesday before Easter, and he had a lot on his mind and many things to do in preparation for the holiday. In the hustle and bustle, he didn't think about the weather that day.

One of Rev. Cooper's pre-Easter tasks was to give a talk to the youth group that evening. He was surprised to find that the usually rambunctious group of teenagers appeared somber that night. Strangely, when the meeting was over, they didn't rush out as usual, but hung around, saying prayers for their friends and family.

Meanwhile, elsewhere in the sanctuary the choir was in full swing practicing for the Easter Sunday service. Rev. Cooper found that they were reluctant to leave when they finished their practice, too. Rev. Cooper didn't know what to make of it.

A Bible study group met after choir practice, and Rev. Cooper hurried to that.

At about 7 P.M. a knock on the door interrupted the group. Rev. Cooper was beckoned out into the hall, where a congregant told him that two parishioners had called to say there was a tornado on the ground and it was headed in their direction. Rev. Cooper's first thought was, "Well, we're people of faith. We trust in God and we'll just go on with the class." He returned to the room and was about to resume class.

But his second thought was that as a leader he needed to do something. So he closed the Bible and told the study group about the tornado. Everyone in the church—the youth group, the choir, the Bible study group, and a cooking class, as well as some children—gathered in the hallway. There were about seventy people gathered.

Rev. Cooper sent three church leaders outside to look and watch for anything unusual. Everyone else stayed inside, joking and socializing. Like Rev. Cooper, they were used to tornado warnings that amounted to little or nothing. One of the women said, "Let's sing," so they all started singing praise songs.

Rev. Cooper decided to go outside to check on the three people he had sent. There was no wind. The church's big American flag was just hanging straight down. There was no noise—just absolute quiet.

Returning inside, the minister decided to tell everyone to go home. After all, nothing was blowing outside. But a little girl who had a reputation for shyness approached him. "Pastor, the Lord just spoke to me," she said.

"What did He say?" Rev. Cooper asked gently.

"He said to me for you to tell these people that even if this tornado hits this church, that the church will be spared."

Smiling, the minister replied, "Well, God talked to you, not me. You tell them."

Rev. Cooper quieted down his parishioners, and the little girl shyly had her say.

Three or four minutes later, the tornado hit. Had Rev. Cooper done as he had intended when he came inside, had the shy little girl not delayed him, people could have been hurt out in the open.

The men who had been posted outside the church came bursting through the door. One of them said, "It sounds like there's a jet plane that's going to land on this church." He urged them to take cover. At the same time an older man from the back of the church shouted, "It's the tornado and it's here—everybody get down."

The back of the church building had metal on it, and it sounded like a lawnmower was hitting that place on the wall, louder, and louder, and louder. There was a roaring sound, just like a jet plane.

Rev. Cooper yelled at everyone to get down! His wife was in another hallway, connected to the larger one where he was standing. His son was some feet away, about halfway down the room. Some people started screaming—especially the kids and young children. Other people were singing hymns.

The building began to shake. There were two doors between the seventy people and a fellowship hall. These doors flew open. The entire church was shaking.

The walls of the concrete church were beginning to buckle as powerful winds twisted thick beams of structural steel. Then the tornado swept a dozen cars out of the parking lot into a nearby ravine. Somewhere in the church a ceiling crashed down, and all the lights went off.

"You couldn't see anything," Rev. Cooper says. "You just heard people screaming and there were things flying all around you. You could hear those steel girders cracking and giving way. It was terrifying. Doors were pulled off their hinges and went flying down the hallway."

A flying door struck the minister in the head and knocked him down, the door on top of him. Rev. Cooper was lying on the floor, dazed by a blow that could have been fatal. "I think I prayed at that moment, 'Lord save us.' I certainly hope I didn't pray, 'Lord save me.'" He could hear other people praying out loud to be saved.

Rev. Cooper eventually found the strength to push the door off his body. He yelled, "Anybody got a flash-light?" A woman gave him a penlight, and he and a few others started to search the building.

The whole building had been destroyed except for the hallway area where the people had been. Both ends of the hallway had been crushed with debris from the roof, but nothing had fallen down where the people were.

People were cut up and bloody. Others had bruises. But nobody had any broken bones. Rev. Cooper found his seventeen-year-old son sitting on the floor; his whole face was covered with blood. "Daddy, I'm scared," said the boy. That's when Rev. Cooper broke down and cried.

It took only a few moments for the tornado to go on its way. It killed thirty-four people that night, traveling twenty-two miles and causing massive destruction wherever it touched down. But not one person in any church was killed, even though most churches were crowded those days just before Easter. A church located just 200 feet from Rev. Cooper's was not full, however. Services were canceled, because the pastor said the Lord had spoken to him and told him it would be dangerous. One of their buildings was completely destroyed and the other one was badly damaged.

Rev. Cooper says one of his most vivid memories that evening is climbing out a window of the destroyed church with his son and standing outside looking at the building. "God, this is a miracle!" He cried aloud. "Immediately when I said that I heard the Lord speaking to me in my heart and saying, 'It's only the beginning.'"

Rev. Cooper says that some of his parishioners who were not present that night have told him, "I wish I had experienced a miracle." He tells them, "To experience a miracle you've got to have a distressing time—that's what I had and I wouldn't want to repeat it."

But that following Easter Sunday, hundreds of parishioners gathered outside of their tornado-damaged church to praise God and celebrate the miracle they believe took place there. They stood solemnly in a parking lot strewn with debris from the destroyed building and listened to Rev. Cooper talk about a tornado that had left thirty-four people dead but had miraculously spared their lives. It was a celebration of small miracles, unbroken spirits, and the promise of renewal.

*F*our-year-old Brayden Hembree is a "miracle from God," declares his mother, Cher, who in February of 2000 was virtually certain she had lost her two-year-old to pneumonia that had destroyed both of the boy's lungs.

On February 19 of that year, the two-year-old was rushed to South Carolina's Laurens County Hospital with a fever of more than 105 degrees. Cher, who was separated from her husband at the time, was living with her son in Clinton, South Carolina, and working in the day care center Brayden was attending.

Brayden had been sick for three weeks, and the family doctor was treating him with antibiotics. But he wasn't getting any better. In addition to his rapidly climbing fever, the child's breathing was troubled. The family doctor told Cher to bring Brayden to the emergency room.

Cher first became frightened that something was seriously wrong when she and Brayden didn't have to wait in the emergency room, but were seen immediately by a battery of doctors.

X-rays of Brayden's lungs revealed bilateral pneumonia—fluid in both lungs. He received Nebulizer (breathing) treatments and was fed oxygen through a face mask. The hospital ran test upon test on Brayden, finally concluding that he had suffered an allergic reaction to the mold and mildew in his bathroom at home.

Brayden was admitted to the hospital, and the very next morning his lips and fingernails had a blue tint to them, which suggested respiratory failure. He was transferred to the specialized intensive care pediatric unit at a hospital four hours away. During the transport, he slipped into a coma.

The head of the intensive care unit met Cher as soon as she arrived and told her that he didn't know if Brayden was going to live or not. She called everyone in her family to ask for prayers.

Praying in times of need comes naturally to Cher and her family. Born and raised in South Carolina, church was always mandatory in her religious Pentecostal household.

All that night, Cher and her parents and other family members who had come to the hospital were down on their knees praying. The next morning, Brayden was still alive, but none of the doctors were optimistic.

Three weeks passed and Brayden was still in a coma. Cher and her family now grew hopeful that he would survive. But their fear grew again when they learned that Brayden had developed a hole in his lung and doctors had to insert a chest tube. Eighteen more chest tubes had to be inserted over the next few weeks. Brayden's blood pressure kept going up. His fever was so high that the doctors directed he be packed in ice.

There were more questions than answers about Brayden's condition. An EEG showed abnormal brain activity, so the doctors thought he might have suffered some brain damage. But there was no way to know until he came out of the coma.

Brayden's doctor told Cher that her son was getting worse and there was nothing more they could do for him. He had concluded that the pneumonia was viral and not bacterial, and could not be treated by an antibiotic.

The doctor had consulted with a larger hospital in

Charleston about Brayden, but they had nothing to offer and didn't think he would survive a transport to that hospital, anyway.

More holes were developing in the boy's lungs. Exploratory surgery disclosed there were so many holes that the doctors doubted they could patch them all. Nonetheless, they would attempt the patching, though they told Cher her son was likely to die in the few days following. Even if Brayden survived the surgery, he would be in the hospital for up to one and a half years.

Cher and her family kept praying for Brayden. And a woman who worked with Cher's grandmother started an Internet prayer chain in the beginning of March. "It was really incredible to know that so many people were praying for us—it really exploded," says Cher.

Cher believes that this explosion produced the miracle.

Brayden came out of his long sleep on his second birthday, on March 16. He weighed only thirty-five pounds, and he couldn't walk or sit up but was breathing on his own.

When Cher rushed to Brayden's room, he reached toward her, crying. He hadn't yet recovered his powers of speech. When she came to him, he pointed at the ceiling. Cher looked up, there was nothing there—no light fixture or mark. Cher has asked Brayden about this since, but he was so little he doesn't remember. She

believes her son was seeing someone invisible and benev-
olent. Maybe God, or an angel.

When Cher asked the doctors what accounted for
her son's recovery, most shrugged, but one admitted that
he considered it a miracle.

For Brayden has no brain damage. His lungs have
recovered completely—he doesn't even have the asthma
he was predicted to have, and a lung function test two
years later showed perfectly normal functioning. He has
been walking normally since two weeks after he left the
hospital. All he has left are scars on his chest—marks
that the four-year-old sometimes points to, saying, "these
are my boo-boos and God healed me."

*C*ountry music star Marty Raybon always seemed to have everything going for him—from a lucrative recording career with his award-winning band, Shenandoah, to plenty of money, to a beautiful wife and a loving family.

However, what looked good on the outside was different on the inside. What Marty's fans did not know is how the performer struggled with the emptiness of his existence because he felt like a "hell-bound pagan."

What his admirers also didn't know about was his mother's diagnosis with cancer and how much that tore him apart, or about the bitter lawsuit with his former best friends involving the use of Shenandoah's name. Nor did they know how many times Marty turned to the bottle rather than the Bible to try to cope with his rapidly disintegrating world.

Born and raised in Sanford, Florida, Marty grew up with two brothers and two sisters and parents who were devout Christians in the Southern Baptist faith. "I was only six years old when I pledged myself to God," he relates, "but I certainly didn't keep that promise."

Marty says he "just kind of scuffled through things more or less. I didn't know the first thing about having a relationship with God."

As he grew older, Marty found himself sustained by music. It was his whole life. He sang and played guitar with his father and two brothers in the family bluegrass ensemble. The bluegrass ensemble won all sorts of talent contests, including the Florida State Bluegrass Competition for five consecutive years. Eventually, he decided to head on to Nashville to go after bigger opportunities.

Life changed dramatically for the entertainer when he arrived in Nashville. This was the big city with its big-city temptations. "I was self-centered instead of God-centered back in those days," he says regretfully. "Ambition guided me more than God." Unable to make it in the Nashville music scene, hungry and poor, Marty decided to leave Nashville for Muscle Shoals, Alabama, to check out a new country music scene.

There he hooked up with several other struggling musicians, forming Shenandoah. Just two short years after the band was formed, success struck. Shenandoah was now hitting the charts, and money was starting to pour in.

"It was great to be on top of the country music charts," he recalls, "but there was a price to pay." Marty had started drinking when he was fifteen. "I was drinking, carousing, lying—you name it and I was guilty of it. I was a hell-bound pagan before I experienced a miracle in my life and fell in love with Jesus."

By now, Marty was married and had children, but he was neglecting his family life. "I was running away from the Lord," he professes. "The whole world had gotten hold of me instead of God and I knew it.

"I'm not even going to get into what drinking and staying gone all the time playing music can do to a family," he says. "And although I was good to my young'uns and to my wife, when you're drunk you don't have to beat a woman to hurt her. You can abuse a woman with your tongue."

Marty says that all the time he felt "the Lord pulling on me" but resisted. But he found that the harder he ran from God the more he felt the pull.

It was on one March morning in 1991 that Marty hit rock bottom. He awakened in the basement of his house with a severe hangover, still drunk at 11:30 in the morning. "I was burnt to a frazzle, at my rope's end. This was in my home in Alabama and, brother, I was really feeling like a hell-bound pagan."

Marty recalls that when he glanced at his reflection in the mirror, the face staring back at him filled him with revulsion. He knew that the booze was going to wreck his health, his career, and his marriage.

Then came the miraculous moment. "I just felt the Lord in my heart," says Marty. "It was this incredible overwhelming feeling. Then I fell down on my knees and prayed. I told the Lord I wanted a chance to raise my young'uns in His way. I told Him that I couldn't go on one more minute, one more hour like this. I told Him that I was scared that I was going to die and that I was going to die without Him."

Marty can only describe what happened to him that morning in his basement as a "miracle." It changed his entire life. "I came to Him with a heart as humble as a child," he recalls. "I said, 'Lord, I'm as stripped down as I can be. I'm as low as I can get. Father, more than anything else in the world, I know that unless I change I'm gonna die without you. What I need, Lord, is you.'"

In the midst of his plea, Marty felt the spirit of the Lord come over him, and he realized that he knew the goodness of God. "That morning I was at the Jordan River and I became the Christian I am today."

Marty asked God to make him a better husband and a better father, to take away the drinking and the yearning for cigarettes. "I asked him to make me a better witness for the Lord."

Marty climbed the basement stairs to the bedroom where his wife, Melonie, lay sleeping. Gently, he woke her and told her what had happened to him.

"I told her what had happened to me in that basement—about the miracles I had experienced. I also told her that we were going to start to go to church. I'll never forget the tears in Melonie's eyes as she listened to what I had to say, and how gratefully she embraced me. This was another miracle—the healing of my marriage."

Marty says there have been many trials in his life since that day, and even more temptations. But everything that he prayed for in that basement has come to pass, Marty attests. He has never had a drink or smoked again, and he hasn't longed for either one. He adds that miracles come once in a lifetime and vows made during such moments should be kept sacred. "No matter what has happened to me—from my mother's cancer to my legal problems—I have never forgotten my pledge to God. He gave me a miracle and I'm giving back. Everything I do, I do as a vessel of the Lord. He led a hell-bound pagan like me out of sin, and I will never forget that."

*J*eanna Cannarozzo candidly admits that for many years she was involved in countless bad relationships in search of her future husband. She grew so weary of pursuing dead-end relationships that one day she finally turned it all over to God.

"I told the Lord that I didn't care if another man ever looked at me again," she relates. "I didn't want anymore jerks. I stopped actively looking and totally submitted to God, trusting Him to bring the one He wanted for me, instead of looking for myself.

"I've always loved religion," Jeanna declares. She was

saved when she was ten. She admits there were some ups and downs in her spiritual life, but "when I got into my twenties and experienced some hardships, that's when I permanently turned back to God." She was in her mid-twenties when she first began to pray for a husband.

Now in her thirties, giving it up completely to God, Jeanna decided to help God out by making a list of exactly the traits and characteristics she wanted in a husband.

A Christian, preferably Baptist;
Living close to her home in Atlanta, Georgia;
Of Italian descent with dark, curly hair;
Who had lived in the New York area;
Employed in the financial field;
Must be wonderful and think she was too;
Must be extremely attractive and attracted to her;
Must be a sweet, outgoing, and strong man;
Should drive a Nissan (Jeanna says it's a long story as to why this was on her list).

A friend of hers had told her, "You've got to tell God exactly what you want, otherwise, how are you going to know who's right for you?" It made sense to Jeanna. She laughs when she says, "No wonder it took God until I was thirty-six to bring me my soul mate."

Jeanna continued to attend singles events after surrendering the search to God, but she never felt the same sense of urgency. Although several years went by and her soul mate failed to appear, she never lost her faith or trust in God. "I had made my peace with God and I felt free."

Jeanna's faith would be vindicated on December 6, 1998. It was a rare day when she had to work at her job as a legal assistant on a Sunday, but her employer allowed her to come in at noon so she could go to church first and attend a singles Sunday school class.

The class had a band and the music was loud. Jeanna remembers thinking that she was getting really tired of the singles scene. "I decided right then and there that I would never marry," she said.

She would concentrate on worshiping the Lord and take classes where she could learn and grow. She could accept that it wasn't in God's plan for her to get married.

Jeanna hated to think of what her relatives would say. But she thought, *Well, I've gotten this far with my life and I don't owe anybody an explanation*. She felt a peace come over her. She decided she would never return to this Bible study class.

But she'd sit through this time. The class was structured with an assembly and then smaller study groups. After the assembly, she headed to the restroom and then returned to the refreshment table for a cup of water. On the way, she noticed a very handsome man leaning against a chair sort of looking out at the room.

Jeanna's about five foot two and she'd always focused on guys who were five ten, but this man was about five six. Still, she thought, he was cute.

Jeanna reminded herself she wasn't going to start anything. She was burned out on dating, and marriage was not in her future. She turned away from him. She had her Bible in one hand and purse in the other as she was trying to get a glass of water. Then she heard a voice say, "You need some help with that?" She looked up and it was him, with a big grin on his face.

Jeanna suddenly heard a voice, from nowhere. Whether it was in her head, an angel, or the Holy Spirit speaking to her heart she'll never know. It said simply, "This is from God." She and the handsome man just stood there looking at each other, mesmerized.

"I just knew instantly that there was something very special about him. It was a feeling I had never known before," says Jeanna.

They stood there talking, oblivious that everyone had gone to their classes. They went to class together, still talking. "The poor Sunday school teacher!" says Jeanna.

Later, Lenny would tell Jeanna that he had noticed her sitting by herself, thought she was cute, and really wanted to meet her. He had recently gone through a divorce and was also eager to begin a new relationship.

When she disappeared into the ladies' room, Lenny had gotten anxious. "That's just my luck," he thought. "She's gone. I can't win for losing." When she reappeared, he bulldozed his way through people just to meet her. Lenny had only been in Atlanta for eight months. He was planning to begin searching for a job in Nashville the day after he met Jeanna, feeling that Atlanta hadn't worked out.

But when Lenny and Jeanna started dating, Lenny decided he might like Atlanta after all. Eight months later, the two of them were engaged, and a year from the day they met, Jeanna and Lenny tied the knot. Their Sunday school teacher, who had just gotten ordained, officiated, having forgiven them for talking all the way through Bible study class.

And what about the list of specific traits that Jeanna wanted from the man she was searching for and had presented to the Lord? "Oh, that!" She laughs.

It was clearly a match made in heaven. Lenny is a full-blooded Italian from Buffalo, New York. He's an accountant/financial planner, a Christian, and drove a Nissan at the time he and Jeanna met. He's very outgoing and easy to like, and he loves Jeanna's cats. "Most of all," says Jeanna, "he loves me more than I thought anybody could and I love him back the same way. It's truly the love of God."

*L*inda Richardson first met her husband, Paul, a handsome sawmiller, in 1973 at age eighteen, when she and her mother moved from Alabama to Missouri. Linda and Paul were married a year later and soon had children.

Linda and Paul were working at a local factory and June 27, 1982, was the first day of their vacation. Their four-year-old and their eighteen-month-old were at home with Linda's mother, so they went straight to the bar to have a drink.

Linda had two beers. Paul had a few more, and they

headed home. It was a warm summer night around 6 P.M. when they left the tavern. As they drove down Highway 53 in Poplar Bluff, Linda noticed a pack of dogs on the road going off into the fields. She will never know if one of the dogs caused the accident because she was looking at her husband, engaged in conversation.

A few minutes later Paul swerved the car and lost control of it. He had been driving at about seventy-five miles per hour. All Linda can remember is the sound of squealing tires and feeling sure they were going to die. The car hit a ditch and they flipped end over end. Paul's window was all the way down and he was thrown halfway out of it. When the car flipped a final time, it landed on top of his head.

Upon regaining consciousness, Linda found herself upside down and sprawled along the inside windshield. She grabbed his arm, saying, "We gotta get out of here." But Paul wasn't moving. He was still sitting in his seat upside down with his head and shoulder out the window and partially under the car.

Climbing out a window, Linda painfully crawled up an embankment. She was running down the road and a truck came along. Other cars stopped. Some men lifted the car up and pulled Paul out from under. He was bleeding from his eyes, ears, nose, and mouth. They couldn't find a pulse and Linda was certain her husband was dead.

When medical help arrived, Paul was transported by ambulance to the local hospital emergency room. Meanwhile, Linda had lapsed into unconsciousness from the pain.

When she awoke in the emergency room, the first thing Linda remembers hearing is the doctor's voice. "He told me with no mercy whatsoever that he didn't think my husband was going to make it."

Linda and her mother were allowed to see Paul. It was a grim sight. He was unconscious and his body was black from the top of his head to his toes. He was bleeding internally, but the doctors weren't sure from where.

Paul was airlifted to nearby Missouri Methodist Central Hospital, where there was a specialized neuro-surgical ward. He flatlined twice during the ride, and the paramedics resuscitated him. Linda's mother drove her to the hospital. She was shocked and dazed, but along the way, they passed a little funeral parlor. It brought Linda back to consciousness, and she thought, "Dear God, my husband is going to die." She began to pray, and from that moment on, never stopped.

When Linda arrived at the hospital, a nurse immediately summoned the surgeon who was treating her husband. The surgeon took her directly to the prayer room. Following him, Linda was sure her husband was dead. But he said, "Your husband is alive, but let's pray." Then he told her all that was wrong with Paul.

"There's some good news, but the bad news is worse. Your husband has a head injury that no man can live with. He has a basilar skull fracture that stretches from his left temple to the top of his spine. His brain has swelled to the extent that the skull is separated one-and-a-half inches. There's a severe bruising of the brain and cerebral fluid is leaking from him."

The doctor told Linda that if he could not stop the cerebral fluid from leaking, there was a 99-percent chance spinal meningitis would set in and that would kill him. Paul had lost a lot of blood, and the doctors still couldn't determine the source of some of his internal bleeding. Even if Paul managed to survive surgery, he would likely be paralyzed and live out his life in a vegetative state.

Feeling sick to her stomach, Linda asked the doctor what the good news was. "Your husband's still alive," he said, and walked away. Linda and her mother went into Paul's room to see him, and he was still unconscious. He had never had a moment's consciousness since the accident.

But as the two women stood by his bedside, Paul

opened his eyes. "What happened?" he asked Linda. "You don't know? We were in a car wreck," Linda told him.

"Our car's all torn up?" said Paul. Linda couldn't believe that a man in this condition was concerned about a car.

At that very next moment, Paul sat straight up in his bed and began gasping for air. Then he fell back, unconscious. He had flatlined again. Nurses and doctors rushed in, pushed Linda and her mother out of the room, and went to work. They brought him back again.

Linda and her mother started making phone calls. Soon there were prayers being said for Paul at churches in four different states. And then the miracles began to unfold.

Within twenty-four hours Paul's condition had changed dramatically. The next morning he was awake and the only symptom he was reporting was a terrible headache. Within forty-eight hours he was considered to be in serious condition—a step up from critical. Within sixty hours he went from serious to stable and was moved from the neurotrauma unit to a private room.

One day in the hospital's recovery room Paul told Linda about the one thing he clearly remembered from his ordeal: talking to God. Paul was not a religious man, and he didn't see any bright lights or dark tunnels, but there was a point when he felt strongly that God was close by him.

All the pain just went away. Paul told Linda, "It was so peaceful being with God that I just wanted to stay there—I didn't want to come back to the pain." Linda believes this memory was one of the times when Paul flatlined.

Within seven days of coming into the hospital by helicopter, Paul went home, fully recovered. The bleeding had stopped, the crack in his skull had begun closing, and his bones were all healing. There was no paralysis, no damage to his brain. He came home on his birthday.

Since the accident, Linda and Paul have become committed Christians. For Linda, it is a homecoming: she was raised in a religious home, and, she says, "I always knew that God was real."

Paul was saved a year after he left the hospital. Drinking is no longer an issue in the Richardsons' marriage. "Now I go to church all the time, and I've asked the Lord to come into my life," Linda proclaims. "We couldn't live without Him."

andy McEwen was thirty-one years old when he began having problems with his eyesight.

The first doctor he saw for the condition noted pressure behind his eyes and sent Randy to the hospital immediately for an emergency CAT scan. Randy had to stay overnight in the hospital and have a spinal tap, blood work, and other tests run. The doctors at first suspected he had multiple sclerosis, but more testing and four eye specialists yielded inconclusive results.

Randy went to the eye clinic at Emory University

Hospital in Atlanta. There, he was diagnosed with a rare hereditary disease that, the doctors said, would eventually make him blind. In his case, it might be soon, because his eyesight seemed to be deteriorating at a rapid pace. Most people with his disease go blind so slowly that they don't notice until they have had it for a very long time.

But Randy had lost 90 percent of the peripheral vision in his left eye and 10 percent in his right eye within two months of first noticing the symptoms. The nerves going to his eyes from his brain were under enormous pressure, which was causing them to burst, then calcify. This would, in turn, cause more nerves to burst.

The specialists told Randy that his peripheral vision would go first, and eventually only his central vision would remain. They could offer neither surgery nor medication. His disease, a rare one, had not been studied much.

Randy says he wasn't much bothered. "I just knew in my heart there was a reason God was putting me through this." He felt at peace. Randy had always had a personal connection with God. "I was always close to Him inside of me," he attests. "In my heart I always knew there was a 'God,' but I just didn't know who He was."

In spite of that personal connection, Randy had avoided church for years. When he was a child, his family had attended a Baptist church, where he felt looked down upon because he and his family were poor. But now suddenly he felt the need to go.

Randy and his wife attended various church services but could find nothing that really appealed to them. "I wanted to find the church that God wanted me to find," he explains. One of his neighbors invited them to attend Grace Community Church in Rincon, Georgia, and that changed his life.

In just a few minutes, they knew it was the place for them. They were impressed with the youth pastor and the upbeat music used during services. Pastor Wesley Corbitt's message was plain and simple, and Randy and his wife knew in their hearts it was the right answer.

Randy felt a sense of peace more powerful than he'd ever felt before. "I had had a taste of that peace before, but nothing quite like this," he says, referring to his earlier relationship with God, and his lack of upset over his diagnosis. Any remaining worry about his impending blindness was gone. He was completely available to comfort his family—his wife, his mother, his brothers, and his kids.

Randy recalls that although his pastors, the elders of the church, and members of his church prayed continuously for his recovery, he rarely prayed on his own behalf. When he did offer up prayers for himself, Randy asked for salvation not for his eyes but for his soul.

"This spiritual vision that God gave me was far more beautiful and valuable to me than anything else I had—including my physical vision, my hearing, and my speech, my arms—anything!"

Randy's eyesight was worsening. "I would have rather gone blind and deaf than lose one drop of what I felt in my heart for God," he avows. "All I prayed for was that I could continue to touch the lives of others." More visual examinations followed. Emory University was a teaching hospital, and because of the rareness of his condition, there were many pictures and tests. In November of that year, Randy's eye specialist scheduled him for yet another examination. What concerned him the most at the time was that if his eyesight became even one percent worse his driver's license would be revoked.

Randy was sitting at one of those visual testing machines when the miracle occurred. Randy's vision was restored.

The technician noticed before Randy did. "Why are you here?" she asked seriously.

The specialist came in and confirmed the results of the test: Randy's eyes were 100 percent recovered. His weaker eye, which had been 20/20 before the disease set in, was now 20/15. The pressure behind his eyes, which had been so serious, was better than normal.

Randy laughs when he describes the scene. "No

one at the medical office could believe the results. The technician who gave me the test was in total disbelief. The doctor was completely dumbfounded. He had this blank look on his face. I was praising God and saying, 'He healed me, He healed me,' but the doctor had nothing to say."

Randy proclaims that he is "living proof that miracles happen. I've been asked the question a lot about why God performed this miracle on me and not others. I really can't answer that. All I can say is that I know that God is still in the miracle business, and I know that He is still watching and waiting."

It was February 2002, and rodeo star Cody Custer was in St. Louis in a major bull-riding championship event. He was riding a bull for about seven seconds when all of a sudden the bull turned back at him. The bull hit him in the head with his horn, and Cody saw stars and fell off.

Because the bull stepped on both of his hands, the rodeo doctor had to put a couple of stitches into his riding hand. What Cody didn't realize yet was that his hand was broken.

By evening, the pain in Cody's hand had gotten

worse. So he paid another visit to Dr. Tandy Freeman, the rodeo doctor. Cody's hand was swollen and it was evident that a bone in his hand was moving strangely. There were no x-rays available on site, but Dr. Freeman and, afterward, the orthopedic surgeon he was sent to, both were in agreement: Cody had broken his ring finger.

A makeshift cast was applied to Cody's hand; then Dr. Freeman sent him back to his hotel room for some rest instructing him to report back tomorrow. Meanwhile, he was to stay off bulls.

Cody dropped in at the rodeo Bible study group at the hotel instead of going quietly back to his room.

His friend Chad Denton was there, and Chad called on everyone to pray for Cody's hand. "I believe that if we all pray over Cody's hand it'll be healed—that God'll be with us."

Cody recollects offering no argument. "I said, 'Heck, yeah, that's a good idea,' because I was sitting there feeling kinda sorry for myself." He had asked Jesus into his life at the age of nineteen, and had really been living as a Christian since his marriage. Everyone took their hats off and laid hands on the area where the bone was broken.

Back in his room, Cody called his wife, the mother of their three children, and told her everything. She reminded him that, as a believer, he knew that God *could* heal him—that it was in the Almighty's power to work such a miracle. "But do you believe that God *will* do this for *you?*" she asked. Cody told her he didn't know. His hand still hurt when he went to bed.

But the following morning, the pain seemed less. It was a Sunday and Cody went to a church service in Illinois. The pastor had invited the cowboys to speak, and afterward he anointed them all with oil and prayed over them. Then Cody went back to the rodeo.

Cody can't explain why, back at the rodeo, he decided to remove his makeshift cast. He was amazed to find that the hand with the broken finger looked perfectly normal. "There was no swelling in it at all, no pain, and no broken bone," he declares. So Cody decided to ignore his doctor's advice. He rode two bulls that afternoon and didn't feel a thing.

Later in the day, Cody went to the doctor. When Cody told him what had happened, the doctor shrugged and said, "all right." Dr. Freeman was a believer himself. He ordered an x-ray just to be sure, but he could see there was absolutely nothing wrong with Cody's hand.

Cody went looking for his cowboy friends. "When I told them what had happened, they praised God and whooped with joy," he says.

Cody says he is certain beyond doubt that God healed him so that he could spread the word about the

Lord's healing powers. "I know that you can't put God in a box and make Him do anything He doesn't want to do, because God does what He wants."

His wife's question the night before he was healed was pivotal for Cody: "Do you believe that God will do this for you?" He realized that he did believe, though he hadn't known it at the time.

"God is a personal God, not some abstract notion," Cody says. "And He wants us to be personal with Him — to come to Him and really have a relationship with Him. So if you're hurt, that's the key ingredient. You can read the Bible about all the miracles that were done, but you've got to believe that it can also happen to you."

The first time the Virgin Mary appeared to Linda Russo was in the early 1990s, at a party at her friend Gary's house. She had brought him a relic of St. Jude for a gift. Linda, who was brought up as a strict Roman Catholic, knew that St. Jude is the patron saint for hopeless cases, and Gary was having a lot of problems with his career. Gary burst into tears when he saw the relic, saying that it was the most thoughtful gift anyone had ever given him. "It cost me only eighty-seven cents," Linda admits, but it was clear that the thought behind it had struck home.

Linda photographed the party with a newly purchased disposable camera. She asked Gary to take one of
her, and when the picture came back, the Blessed Mother
was standing right next to her, a white apparition
standing on a cloud. The figure filled half of the photo.

Having been raised a Catholic, Linda says she was
familiar with stories of the Virgin Mary making appear-
ances throughout the world, but she had never expected
to see the Blessed Mother at a party. At first Linda
assumed that someone at the camera store had played a
practical joke on her, so she went to the store to question
the manager.

The manager agreed that the image on the photograph resembled the Virgin Mary, but he thought that
the camera had probably been opened, exposing the film
to light. Linda knows she never opened the disposable
camera. The manager just shook his head. Linda next
showed the print to her local priest, who said it was defi-
nitely the image of a woman, "but I'm not going to say
it's the image of the Blessed Mother."

But two women who worked in the parish office
became nearly hysterical upon seeing the photograph,
shouting, "My God, it's the Blessed Mother! It's the
Blessed Mother!"

A second priest, Rev. Patrick Connolly of New
York City's St. Catherine of Siena Church, also felt

sure the image was Mary. "Father Connolly was an old-fashioned, strict priest," Linda emphasizes. "He wouldn't say this just to placate me."

Linda never knew why the Virgin had appeared to her this way, but it wasn't the last time.

~

A year later, Linda was on a pilgrimage to a farm near Conyers, Georgia, thirty miles east of Atlanta.

The Virgin Mary has visited Nancy Fowler, the owner of the farm, more than sixteen times. Thousands of Catholics flock to the farm every year hoping to catch a glimpse of Mary.

Linda and her friend Luz decided to visit the room where the apparition had been seen. Hundreds of other pilgrims were waiting in a slow-moving line to see the shrine.

As the line approached the entrance to the house, Luz suggested that the two of them pray before entering the apparition room. Linda had a very special string of black rosary beads with her. They were more than 120 years old and had once belonged to her great-grandmother.

As Linda placed the beads across Luz's open palms, an amazing transformation took place. It seemed as if an unseen can of gold spray paint was spraying the beads, transforming them from black to gold very, very slowly right before their eyes.

The two women stared. "Right there, a quarter of an inch off the beads, in the air, this gold spray was coming down like powder—like angelic dust. It went on the prayer beads and on our hands."

It was broad daylight. Linda and Luz got down on their knees and began praying. Linda showed the beads to a man and his wife who were standing on line behind her, and they saw, too, that the rosary was now solid gold.

When she returned to New York City, Linda had the beads assayed. The black rosary beads that had been in her family for more than a hundred years were now solid gold. The assayer thought it was obvious that the beads had never been anything but gold.

Linda now carries the miracle rosary around with her. For the second time in her life, Linda was left wondering why she was the recipient of a miracle visit from the Virgin Mary. "All I can think of is that the Virgin wants me to go on a mission to convert people—to testify about God's presence on earth," she submits. "I think I was shown the photograph and the beads as tools to help me in my mission because I'm not a very good speaker. What better proof than to be able to show people these things?"

*E*lla Brunt and her six-year-old son, Cody, her eight-year-old daughter, Brittany, and her twenty-five-year-old nephew, Wallace, decided to beat the Texas heat by doing a little sailing at nearby Clear Lake on a sunny day one July.

Wallace had sailed his twenty-foot sailboat for years. From the lake, they'd be able to see the new house Ella and her husband were building nearby.

Ella packed a sack lunch, and lots of snacks. They were all excited. As Ella remembers it, the last thing her husband said to her that morning before he left for work was "Don't forget to take along a life jacket."

The temperature was in the upper nineties as they took off, and the wind was high. A man in a motorboat offered to tow them away from the dock. Once away from the dock, Wallace began to raise the sails. He was in front of the boat just finishing putting up the sail when a huge gust of wind hit.

All of a sudden the boat started to capsize. Wallace was on the same side of the boat as Brittany, and he grabbed her.

But no one was near enough to Cody to grab him. The next thing Ella remembers is finding herself in deep water, helplessly watching as Cody got sucked underwater. She could see that everyone else was safe. Her kids all knew how to swim.

But Cody got tangled up in the ropes from the boat. He was thrashing and kicking, trying to get free. Wallace handed Brittany off to Ella, and the two treaded water together while Wallace swam over to Cody and tried to get him loose.

In her dreams, Ella still sees her son surfacing, then being dragged under by the ropes. Wallace dove and dove for Cody. A couple of times he found Cody under the boat, but he couldn't pull him loose from the ropes. Ella kept shouting at Wallace, "Keep trying. You gotta keep trying." He did.

Holding on tightly to Brittany, Ella said, "Brittany, something is very wrong. Let's pray to God."

Turning to God for help was a natural response for Ella. Born and raised in the small oil refinery town of Bay, Texas, Ella regularly attended Baptist and Assembly of God churches on Sundays with her parents and two older brothers. She describes her family as devout Christians, and can recall her father often talking about miraculous healings and other supernatural events around the dinner table.

"We were raised to believe that God still healed today, and that miracles weren't a thing of the past," she professes, "and so as I grew older I never really stopped believing in miracles.

"We're a spirit-filled family and despite all that was going on I tried to put aside all my fears," she relates. "As a mother, my natural instinct was to panic. But I felt at that moment there was a choice I had to make. I could either become hysterical or rely on the Lord." She put aside all fear and concentrated on prayer.

Ella suddenly felt a supernatural peace come over her. She knew that anyone who was under water for as long as Cody had been might suffer brain damage. Ella prayed that if Cody needed emergency medical attention, it would all turn out for the good and do him no harm.

And then suddenly Ella experienced a horrific

vision—one that she believes was an attack by Satan in an effort to turn her away from God when she was most vulnerable. She saw herself holding hands with Brittany and her husband, Ted, as they walked down a path. At the end of the path was a casket, and Ella knew that Cody was in it.

Ella struggled to remember her Bible. She started repeating the verses that described Jesus' defeat of Satan, and the vision disappeared as quickly as it had appeared.

Instantly, that feeling of God's peace engulfed her again. She felt, inexplicably, that everything would be okay. And she saw that Wallace was emerging from the water with Cody in tow. By now, her son had been trapped under the boat for about seven minutes.

Cody was draped over Wallace's shoulder, limp. His limbs were lifeless; his color was blue. Suddenly Ella knew that he was dead. There was no way he could have survived being underneath that boat for so long.

It seemed like an eternity before other people on the water realized what was happening and arrived to offer help. A Jet-Skier took Brittany back to shore and called for help. Ella told her daughter, "Brittany, you've gotta keep praying."

Emergency medical help arrived soon afterward, and the still-unconscious Cody was airlifted to Herman

Hospital in Houston. He did not respond to CPR, and he never regained consciousness on the way to the hospital.

Because there was no room for her in the helicopter, Ella had to make the long trip to the hospital through rush-hour traffic. When she arrived, her husband, Ted, was already there waiting for her. By the look on his face, Ella knew the news was not good.

A doctor came and gave her the news. There was no question that Cody's brain was damaged. His lungs were bleeding internally, and the doctors couldn't stop it. Within a couple of hours Cody's brain would begin to swell, and they would have to drill holes in his skull to relieve the pressure.

For three days the six-year-old boy lay in a coma in the hospital, depending on life support. His condition continued to deteriorate. The doctors and the staff didn't expect him to live. "I felt as if my heart was being ripped out of my body," Ella remembers.

Members of her family had gathered in the waiting room to conduct a constant prayer vigil. "We were trying to be strong and hold on," she recollects, "but I think we all realized there was only one option left for us—a miracle."

Ella never once stopped praying. She still remembered the feeling she had in the lake. She would remain as positive as she could. She listened politely to the doctors' grim daily reports, but she believed that while the doctors were treating Cody's body, God was responsible for a lot more.

Ella and her family determined not to speak anything but faith-filled words. They took a recent picture of Cody and taped it over his bed. Anytime anyone would come into his room, Ella would say, "You see that picture? Cody will walk out of this hospital ward one-hundred percent whole and looking just like you see him in that picture."

Cody's doctors said he was dying. Pneumonia had set in, along with a host of infections. Ella couldn't sleep, haunted as she was by the images of Cody on the lake, emerging and being dragged under. There were times when she wept and yelled at God to please help.

But the prayers of her family, friends, and church members always helped to pick her up. "I could literally feel those prayers," she says. Five days after Cody's admission to the hospital, the life support machines were still showing that his lungs were wiped out. The next day, Cody's doctors removed some of his breathing tubes. Cody started breathing on his own. He was still unconscious.

Later that same day, one of Cody's doctors was in his room writing up a report. Although he was nonresponsive, she spoke to the boy. The doctor almost dropped her pen when Cody replied, "Yes, ma'am."

Cody's eyes were open. Two days later, he was off the ventilator. There was no evidence of the irreversible brain damage the tests had shown. Cody had to go to rehab and learn how to eat. His balance was off, and there were other problems that were to be expected after days in a coma.

Every day during Cody's recovery, Ella made a note of any stumbling blocks he had met with that day. Then she'd go home and pray to God to help her son with that specific problem. On the next day, the problem she had noted no longer existed. Cody's recovery was ten days, rather than the six to eight weeks the doctors had projected.

Today, Cody has no lingering health problems. He was an all-star baseball player the summer before entering first grade and has taken up tennis. God has restored him physically, and mentally—in every way.

Some months after his ordeal, Cody recalled being in a coma. "I saw God, back then," he said. "I was in heaven and He stepped out of the bright light and said some things to me—but I just can't remember what." Ella believes that someday, Cody will remember.

*P*aramedic Charles Shepherd had worked in emergency services for more than twenty years, but he had never seen anything like the survival of baby Patrick.

It was on a cold Tuesday in December 2000 in London, Kentucky, that Charles and his partner, Jeff, got a call that there was a tractor-trailer wreck fifteen or so miles out in the country. It was a busy day, with fifteen-degree weather creating black ice. The truck driver had lost control when he hit a patch.

Jeff and Charles were en route when the dispatcher

let them know there was a man climbing through the windshield. "I always pray on every run for the Lord to help me do my job," Charles says, and he remembers praising God that there was at least one survivor.

The dispatcher also told them that a twenty-eight-year-old woman who was eight months pregnant had been fatally thrown from the truck that her husband was driving.

When Charles and Jeff rolled up at the scene, a bunch of people were standing around. The husband was standing next to a blanket. He was agitated and crying.

When Charles pulled back the blanket, he saw a newborn baby, still attached by the umbilical cord to his lifeless mother whose body had been severed in the crash. The husband had pulled it out and wrapped it up with a blanket given to him by a family who lived not far from the highway and had rushed to the scene.

The husband thought the baby was dead, but Charles thought differently. He could feel the baby's heart still beating in the umbilical cord. When he squeezed hard on the umbilical cord, the baby emitted a wail. Charles started to work.

Much of what happened in the next few moments remains a blur. All Charles can remember clearly is keeping his eyes on the infant, who was blue and motionless, while the father, the truck driver, was standing nearby and sobbing hysterically. Charles cut the umbilical cord with scissors, wrapped the infant against the cold, cleaned the baby's nose and mouth with a syringe, and gave it oxygen.

The father bent down over the baby, breathing on him to keep him warm. Another ambulance arrived to transport the father to the hospital, and Charles and Jeff got the baby into the back of their truck, taking him on a fifteen-minute dash to the Russell County Hospital.

During that frantic ride to the emergency room, Charles prayed unceasingly for the baby's recovery. "I prayed more on that run than any I've ever prayed before," he declares. "I said, 'God, please take care of this little guy.'"

Once the baby was safe in the care of the hospital's medical staff, Charles retreated to a little room where emergency services personnel usually did their paperwork. "I went in there and sat down by myself. I kind of leaned my head on the desk and thought, 'God, what have I just seen?' I prayed and kind of let God sit down beside me."

In those quiet moments, Charles experienced a vision. God was speaking to him: "I'm still in control, but sometimes it seems to me like everybody leaves me out—even you. It's December nineteenth and almost

Christmas, and in the hustle and bustle of Christmas I see people focusing on other things than me. But I'm still in control. I give life and I take life and I've done both right here in front of you today."

Charles was overwhelmed. "My heart was hurt by what I had seen and heard that day, and yet I was rejoicing."

After the story was carried by various media throughout the nation—including CNN—Charles was contacted by other paramedics as far away as California who told him they had never heard of something so extraordinary happening to one of their own.

The following day, Charles went to visit the infant and got a chance to talk to the child's father. The baby's father said that when the wreck happened his wife had been thrown through the windshield. She had been in the sleeper and wasn't using the safety net. The truck had run over her, then dragged her some feet. All the young father could see when he got out was the baby's head and arm in a bloody mess. He thought she was delivering the baby so he helped pull it out and covered the baby to keep him warm. He hadn't even seen that his wife was torn in two.

How is it possible that such great tragedy had brought such a miracle? Charles thinks he knows. The Kentucky State Police found something next to the crash—two Bibles. One was lying just a few feet from where the mother was and it was open to John, chapter 20, which depicts Mary Magdalene standing outside Jesus' tomb: "As she wept, she bent over to look into the tomb and saw two angels in white."

~

Charles Shepherd was already a believer in miracles when he rescued Patrick. But it hadn't always been thus. Born in Indiana and raised in Kentucky, Charles says in his younger days any talk about miracles would make him laugh. His mother died when he was fifteen months old and his father wasn't a church-goer until Charles was about fourteen. His father brought Charles to the Baptist church until he was sixteen, but then he and his brothers and sisters "quit" the church. "I thought I knew everything back then, so I didn't give my heart to the Lord until I was twenty-nine."

By age twenty-nine, Charles was married with a four-year-old son. He seemed to have the whole world in his hands until tragedy struck.

First came a divorce and then his son, Eric, was diagnosed with cancer and given little chance of recovery. A few months later Charles's father got sick with brain cancer.

"My dad was in one hospital and my son was across the street in another," Charles says. "Two people in this world whom I loved the most were sick, and I still couldn't even pray for them. I still resisted praying and going to church."

One day at the hospital Charles's cousin asked if anyone wanted to go to the chapel with him to pray for both family members. "Something made me go with him," says Charles. When Charles and his cousin walked into the chapel, there was a Bible open on the podium to the Twenty-third Psalm, "The Lord is my shepherd; I shall not want."

"It just hit me right then," Charles says. "I recognized that God could do all things."

Charles knelt beside his cousin, and they cried together, then prayed, then talked. His cousin asked Charles if he wanted to be saved, and he said he did.

"From that day on I asked the Lord to come into my heart," says Charles. "And He did. Four days later my son got out of the hospital. The doctors didn't think he would live beyond five years old, and today he's twenty and still doing well. My father didn't make it, but my son did. The Lord took my dad and spared my son, and I consider Eric's survival a miracle." From a hospital chapel to a Kentucky highway, Charles believes that God is walking the country keeping a loving eye on things, and he wonders what miracle he will see next.

On a hot August day, Torry Slaton and his brother-in-law were working on a new modular home in the foothills of the Sierra Nevada. It was about 5:30 P.M. and the flies were buzzing around them as they stood twenty-five feet above the ground. They were about to take a break to eat when Torry brushed his eyes to chase away the bugs, and his left contact popped out. Neither one of them could see it anywhere.

Torry's brother-in-law suggested that they pray. So they did, and then looked a little further before climbing down. Torry tried to mark his spot in relation to the ground, and when he looked at the ground, he found the contact lens lying there in the middle of some dirt.

Torry readily admits this falls into the category of a small miracle, but he is not complaining. Still, there was more to come. It was a few months later in November that Torry's family went for a walk in the first big snow of the year. Torry's two-year-old daughter, Tasha, was seated on his shoulders. She swatted his eye with her hand, and his left contact lens popped out again.

The family asked Jesus to help them find the contact lens. "Our family always prays over everything. I feel it's a great teaching tool for our kids to trust in God and when God rewards your faith for the child to see that," says Torry. A few minutes later Torry's wife, Heidi, found the contact in the snow.

The next time was a week later, and Torry was working on his new modular home again. Torry invited a few friends over to help him finish building a snow roof. It was a Sunday and they had been working on the roof all day long. Torry placed a nail with his left hand and swung with his right hand, and hit the nail just under the head. The nail ricocheted back up toward him, and the point of the nail literally hit him dead center in the left eye—the same eye again.

Torry pulled back and closed his eye, painfully. After a few minutes he opened his eye and he realized his contact lens was not in his eye.

For the third time, Torry found himself searching for his missing left contact lens. Heidi came out to help him look.

When she found it in the dirt, Torry's first reaction was, "Oh, I can't use this." There, in the middle of his hard lens, was a hole in the shape of a diamond. Hard lenses usually snap under any sort of pressure.

One of Torry's friends looked at it and said, "Well, talk about providence." As it dawned on Torry what had happened, he says he thought to himself, "Shame on me for not recognizing a miracle." The contact lens had acted like a shield against a bullet. It had saved him from having his left eye pierced by a nail.

Torry emphasizes that he has always believed in miracles. "I was raised religiously in the Seventh-day Adventist Church," he explains, "and I was constantly made aware that miracles do happen. As a youngster, I often read about them in the Bible. I'm still very much interested in the subject and I always read books about people exercising faith in God as I always have. Growing up, my mom put it in my mind to keep in touch with God and I have."

Torry says that if he hadn't found the lens when it popped out a week earlier, he doubts he would have had time to replace it before the accident occurred. His eye would have been bare, and the nail would have struck it.

Torry keeps the contact lens with the diamond-shaped hole in a special case in his desk drawer. It is a reminder to him of the rewards of having faith in God.

*T*ourists driving through Virginia's historic Amelia County often photograph the local Tabernacle United Methodist Church. This picturesque building sits on a hill between two little valleys with woods behind it. The original structure was built before the Civil War, and rebuilt around 1910 with white sideboards. The original pews and other historic details keep the building in touch with its heritage. And though it's just one of many beautiful churches in this area, something special took place here in 1966.

~

The firemen awakened Rev. Steve Parker from sleep about 3 A.M. on the Friday before Easter because the church was burning. By the time the pastor and his wife had rushed to it, the beloved building was almost burned to the ground. The old pine boards burned quickly, and soon nothing more of the old church remained but cement steps leading to charred posts and black soot.

The minister is thankful the church had burned nearly to the ground before local firemen arrived on the scene, for some of them were among his congregation and really cared for it. He didn't want to see anyone risking his or her life. As it was, no one was hurt.

Recalling that terrible morning, standing there with little of the old church remaining, Rev. Parker says he and the others present could only look on in shock and disbelief. "The first thing I thought was, 'What's next? Where are we going from here?'" But then some of his congregants gathered in a circle and prayed with him. "Once we had prayer, we knew which way to go," he says.

The minister asserts that from the moment the prayer session ended, there was no doubt in anyone's mind that this was not the end of the church, but a new beginning. "When can we get started getting it back up?" every congregant said, in different ways.

It began to happen just hours following the fire. A colorful banner hoisted over the remaining front steps of the burned-out church, "Worship, Sunday, 9:45 A.M.," greeted distraught parishioners who came to see the damage. When Sunday came, two days later, greeters were on hand to welcome the church congregation, and hand out bulletins and yellow ribbons.

A local funeral home donated money, and chairs were purchased and placed on the lawn where a tent was erected. Services were held, just like normal, except they were outside. The usual attendance of 30 to 35 people swelled to more than 100 for that day. The pastor discussed the events leading up to the fire and his dreams for new additions to the building—including a fellowship hall and a kitchen. He told everyone they'd be back in full operation by October—just six months away.

The insurance coverage for the church building was far from enough to replace all that had been lost that morning—in the end, the insurance money accounted for about half of the cost of new construction.

In the weeks following the fire, a makeshift pulpit with a wooden cross and pictures of the church was constructed and placed in front of the burned-out building. A pickup truck that had a makeshift sound system with the choir seated off to one side was on hand each Sunday. Churches from as far away as northern Virginia donated hymn books and office equipment. Carpenters, cabinet makers, and other craftsmen worked for deferred payment for the church.

One Sunday soon after the fire, a stranger pulled off the road to see the wreckage. He gave all the money from his wallet—change and all—and donated it to the church. He vowed to come back and give more—and he did!

The fire never interrupted religious services. The pastor's promise of a building by October was ambitious—and only one month off the mark. By the middle of November his congregation was meeting in its new Fellowship Hall, while work was finished on the sanctuary. The Tabernacle United Methodist Church had Sunday school, was offering prayers to the sick, and worshiping the Lord as they always had.

Six years after the disaster, attendance at the Tabernacle United Methodist Church has more than doubled. Rev. Parker praises God for this increase in church attendance. "We have children coming from everywhere in the county, so you can see how God used a disaster to make something great out of it."

But Rev. Parker knew from the first time he surveyed the wreckage of the beloved old building that his church would be just fine. As he walked around surveying the fire early that Friday morning, he saw two white lilies newly planted in front of the church, a symbol of Easter and rebirth, giving him hope. Today, Rev. Parker can only think about what happened here as the miracle of the comeback church.

$\int$he was the daughter of one of the hospital's OB nurses, and she had contracted viral encephalitis (a swelling of the brain). Respiratory arrest and seizure had set in. Doctors at Los Angeles's White Memorial Medical Center, where Pastor Paul Crampton was director of Chaplaincy Services, were convinced that only a miracle could save the child's life.

It was the third day of the little girl's hospitalization and the pastor's phone rang. The OB nursing staff asked him to lead them in a prayer for the little girl and her family. The child had slipped into a coma and was placed on a respirator where the attending physician pronounced a prognosis: She had a 20- to 50-percent chance of survival.

Calls such as this one requesting that the pastor pray are not unusual at the 350-bed hospital, founded by the Seventh-day Adventist Church in 1913. "This is a place where people are willing and free to share their spirituality and give their all for the good of others," says the chaplain. "So I was always being asked for support and prayer."

When Pastor Crampton arrived a few moments later at the nurses' station in the hospital's delivery area, an impressive number of people had gathered—from physicians to housekeeping staff—to support the nurse and her daughter.

The group formed a circle and held hands. After a few moments of prayer, Pastor Crampton took note of something special: a strong, tangible feeling of God's presence. He describes it: "This was more of an experiential thing, and it's hard to explain. I think that all of us who are spiritual have felt from time to time that we are speaking to God, but the words come out feeling like they're hitting the ceiling and not really going anywhere.

"And there are other times when we're speaking to Him and there's this obvious connection. The hair will stand up on your arm and there's this energy that takes place. In this room, that's exactly what was happening. There was a connection to God and a connection among us that you could feel. You could just sense that this was a powerful prayer."

Although the doctors didn't know a miracle had occurred yet, Pastor Crampton is convinced the ailing girl's life was saved during those moments when he and the others were praying in that room.

The doctors were amazed when the little girl opened her eyes a couple of days later. On the fifth day, the respirator was unhooked and she was able to breathe on her own. She was alert and responsive. On the sixth day, she started talking and taking in food, and was able to get up with assistance.

It wasn't long before she was back home with her parents. There was no brain damage, and the girl was back in school very soon after she returned home.

~

Pastor Crampton has another miracle story to tell from the very same hospital.

"There was a woman who was admitted with an aneurysm in her brain, and it got to the point where the medical staff didn't think it was useful to continue with her life support. They asked the husband if he wanted to disconnect the equipment to ease her suffering, and it was very difficult for him to do it."

Pastor Crampton says it was at this point that he got involved in the case. "This man had a very strong faith, and also an understanding that the whole situation was God's will. He was resigned to accepting whatever that will would be. He said he was going to put his wife into God's hands, and he hoped that God would work a miracle. And he asked for prayer, so we prayed with him."

A couple of hours later, the equipment was disconnected. Death was expected in short order. But not only did the woman live, she recovered fully in two weeks and went home. "It was absolutely amazing," says Pastor Crampton. "Nobody in the hospital could believe that had happened because it was almost unheard of. It was really a miracle."

~

What does the hospital chaplain have to say about the nature of miracles? "I just wish I could say they happened more often," he says. "But it's an amazing thing to see them when they do happen. For a long time I've tried to wrap my mind around the question of why miracles don't happen more often. And I still haven't come up with a satisfactory answer.

"You know, miracles don't always have to do with physical healings. There are a lot of other kinds of miracles that take place. There's the miracle of acceptance, miracles of forgiveness, and the miracle of being able to deal with a horrible disease, or a life-threatening illness. There are emotional miracles where people grow close to God under trying circumstances—these types of miracles are also very impressive to me—sometimes even more impressive than a physical healing."

*H*al Weeks was fifty-eight when he discovered he had lymphoma, or cancer of the lymphatic system. He was given a 35-percent chance of survival for five years.

Hal was treated with cobalt for a period of twenty-one days, and for four years after that treatment, every checkup went fine. But then, when Hal was sixty-two, his doctor discovered cancerous tumors on his neck and under his right armpit. He had nodular lymphoma. Chemotherapy was the next step.

To his physician's dismay, Hal declined to call the

oncologist. He needed some time to think things over.

It was just about that time that a friend invited Hal to attend a Full Gospel Businessmen's Fellowship dinner near his home. Hal was a deacon in the Methodist Church, but he had been mainly involved in the business side of things—a nominal Christian, in his own terms. "I was going to church but not really feeling God's spirit," he describes his relationship to God.

That meeting was to change his life forever. "Something happened at that dinner," Hal recalls. "I was prayed for at this dinner and I got baptized in the Holy Spirit. I spoke in tongues. For the first time in my life, I really felt the spirit of God coursing through me."

Something shifted for Hal, and it was soon after that when he offered up the prayer: "Lord, if the religious life is something you want me to get involved in, heal my back," referring to his chronic back trouble. He wasn't ready to ask for a cure for his cancer.

The following Saturday evening Hal developed a strange tingling sensation in his right arm. Then it spread to the side of his face. As he began to rub his face and neck, he felt something like electricity shooting through his right arm.

"Lord, Your hand is holding my hand," murmured Hal. Waves of an indescribable sense of power began to sweep through his entire body.

Hal's back was healed.

Hal hoped that God might heal his cancer as well, and he began to pray for healing. Three months later, during an examination, his doctor looked at him, his face showing confusion. "If I were examining you for the first time, I would have diagnosed you as not having the disease." There was no evidence of the cancer.

Hal wasn't surprised. "From the moment I accepted God into my life at that dinner, I expected healing. I had faith. I just knew that God would heal me."

So two decades later, when Hal's doctor discovered two large lumps over his right collarbone, Hal again refused conventional medical treatment. The lymphoma had returned, but Hal had faith.

For six months, Hal's condition worsened. The tumors increased in size and number. He began to have second thoughts about medical treatment.

It was about 10:30 at night and he was getting ready to go to bed when he heard a voice he knew was the Holy Spirit.

"I thought you had turned it over to me, so why are you doubting my powers?" said the voice. Hal's tumors would be in evidence for three more months, the voice told him, and then disappear.

Hal vowed never to doubt God again. Two months

later, the cancer had stopped progressing. And the next month the tumors were gone.

Hal uses his Web site—*http://howtoheal.org*—to share his testimony and encourage others not to fear illness or death. He gets hundreds of e-mails from people asking him to pray for them. Hal's eighty-nine now, and he teaches weekly Bible classes and holds healing services as well as a weekly prayer healing class where hands-on healing is taught. "I will leave this 'vale of tears' peacefully and without trauma. Who could ask for any more than that?"

*H*ugh Ellis was watching football in his home in Sidney, Michigan, on a late August Sunday afternoon when all of a sudden he heard a loud crunch. He was so engrossed in the game that he ignored it, although he knew there must have been an automobile collision.

A few minutes later there was a banging on the door.

The man at the door told Hugh that a little girl had been hit by a car. Hugh flew out and saw his five-year-old daughter, JoHannah, lying on the cement. Her head seemed to have snapped at the neck. She wasn't breathing and someone who had taken her pulse told Hugh that JoHannah's heart wasn't beating. Witnesses later told the poor father that the girl had flipped up over the vehicle and landed with a crash.

Hugh fell on his knees before her and started praying. "Oh, God, please don't let my daughter die," he cried. Hugh leaned over JoHannah and tried to straighten out her small neck.

Under his touch suddenly there was motion—the five-year-old was unmistakably alive. But Hugh had no time to ponder this impossibility, for the ambulance came and took her to a nearby hospital. From there she would be airlifted to the intensive care unit of Spectrum Hospital in Grand Rapids, where brain injury specialists would care for her.

Hugh and his wife, Deb, were too upset to drive, so a friend drove them to Grand Rapids. Deb and Hugh couldn't so much as speak to each other the whole way down because they were both involved in prayer.

When they arrived at the hospital, the doctor told them that he didn't think JoHannah was going to make it. Hugh and Deb were still silent, not saying anything to each other or to the doctor, lost in desperate prayers.

When the shocked parents were allowed to visit their daughter in the intensive care unit, they were horrified at the sight. "All kinds of tubes and everything else were stuck in her," Hugh recalls. No one expected her to last the night.

But the young girl continued to cling to life. JoHannah survived, albeit in a coma.

After two or three weeks, she started to come out of the coma. Now the doctors were saying they would have to operate on her brain, but that she might not survive the surgery. If she lived, she would be paralyzed for the rest of her life.

Hugh and Deb prayed without ceasing, day and night. Hugh admits that there were moments when he had serious doubts about JoHannah's chances for survival. "I was doubtful in the sense—you know how you think the worst—and thought that I might have a paralyzed daughter on my hands," he submits. "We weren't churchgoers at the time and I didn't have very deep faith. But at the same time I felt that if God could raise the dead, He could also help a little girl."

The surgery was successful. JoHannah had to learn how to crawl, walk, and talk, all over again, but now at eighteen, she's normal and healthy.

The recovery not only transformed Hugh's life, it caused him to become deeply religious. He's in a fellowship at his local church and is considering becoming a pastor. "These days," he says, "I look back at my life and I see that Jesus has been with me every step of the way and that this is a way to return His love."

$\mathcal{R}$abbi Joseph Gelberman was out for a walk in his home town in Hungary in 1939 when he first realized what was brewing in Europe. The children of the community were picking up stones and throwing them at him. "It was a terrible shock," he says.

The next day he was again out for a walk, and a friend who was a Christian clergyman was coming from the other direction. The man passed him in silence with his head averted.

Chilled by this encounter, that night the rabbi talked

things out with his wife. Their daughter was almost two years old, and they knew that for her sake they must try to get to the rabbi's distant relatives in America.

Rabbi Gelberman believes it is a miracle that he even realized he needed to leave the town where he was born. "Something or someone pushed me to come," he attests. "I was never an active person, and yet I had this over-riding sense inside me that said I needed to come to America. Even though things were getting bad, I ordinarily would have stayed close to home. I was like my father—peaceful rather than active. I was not a revolutionary, yet I was pushed by something."

The rabbi discovered that there were thousands of Jews ahead of him also wanting to escape the rising tide of anti-Semitism. The Hungarian government would only allow 200 people to leave for America. Rabbi Gelberman's status as a rabbi allowed him to leave Hungary for a limited time on a non-visa status. The catch was that he would have to leave his family behind.

His family would be allowed to join him if a synagogue in America hired him. "It wasn't an easy decision, but my wife and I decided I should go to America on this chance," he says. "After a long delay this was arranged. We prayed before I left that all would come out well."

The year was 1939 and things did not turn out well at all. One day, the letters from his wife and other members of his family stopped arriving. In addition to his wife and daughter, the rabbi lost his father, his mother, twelve of his sisters and brothers, and many old friends, neighbors, and parishioners. All of the Jews in his home town of Nagyeched, Hungary, had been rounded up by the Nazis and sent to a concentration camp to be killed.

"It was only after the war that I learned all the details of what had happened to them," he relates.

"When I learned the news I broke down, and I was ill for many months. The news almost destroyed me."

But despite the enormous personal tragedy that he suffered, Rabbi Gelberman adds that he has never stopped believing in miracles. To this day the clergy-man remains convinced that his escape from death by the Nazis and arrival in America was nothing short of miraculous.

"I believe it was the miracle of God telling me that I had to save myself—and my family—which I couldn't. And I think part of that miracle was that God had work for me to do in America—to promote religious har-mony." Rabbi Gelberman was one of the few—maybe the first—Hasidic Jews to promote interfaith religious services back in the 1960s.

Rabbi Gelberman's work has been truly inspirational. He serves as the rabbi of "the New Synagogue," and is president of the All-Faiths Seminary in New York

City—a popular interfaith minister-training program. He holds four rabbinical degrees of learning and a Ph.D. in psychotherapy.

Rabbi Gelberman was the first orthodox rabbi to take up yoga. He holds meetings and prayer gatherings with swamis and priests. In 1977, he became the first Hasid to organize a temple bringing East and West together under the spiritual guidance of a swami, a priest, and a rabbi.

"No one had ever heard of a rabbi from the Orthodox tradition doing this before. It was revolutionary and, again, it was way out of my ordinary character. It was not my nature to get involved in things like this. I ordinarily don't respond to things this way. That's why I believe I was guided by God to do all these things. My mission was to help promote religious harmony in His name."

The rabbi believes he was the beneficiary of a miracle of transformation—one that started in 1939 when he felt an urging to leave Hungary for America. "This wasn't a dramatic miracle like God telling Moses he had to get his people out of Egypt right away," he asserts. "This was more gradual.

"There was no heavenly voice in my head saying, 'Go right this moment.' I was just inspired by God or one of His angels to do all of this. And it was a miracle that I could continue to be a joyous Jew and do all the things I did after all that I had suffered with the loss of my family."

He laughs at the memory of his arrival in America. "You know, I didn't even know the language, but one of the first things I did in this country was join the army. It was 1941 and I enlisted for basic training in the infantry. Because I wasn't a citizen, I couldn't be a chaplain. So I said, 'It doesn't matter; I'll be an infantryman.' It was a miracle that I survived three years as a private in the army—sometimes I didn't even understand simple orders. The sergeant would say turn right, and I would turn left."

Rabbi Gelberman's voice becomes solemn as he talks about how he wished some of the miracles he experienced had been passed along to his doomed family members. "They all vanished in a German concentration camp," he says softly.

"I just don't have any answer as to why they had to die. Sometimes there are no answers to these kinds of questions. Why do some people survive and others do not? I'm not enough of an expert to give you an answer. All I can do is continue to believe in God's loving kindness and thank Him for the miracles He has worked in my life over the years."

The rabbi says he has experienced other miracles in

his life as well, such as a complete recovery from an illness that threatened to claim his life. "They happened because my faith in God is so deep," he proclaims. "I have always been able to overcome any kind of pain or tragedy because of this faith."

Rabbi Gelberman, who through his teachings and more than sixty years of ministry has always emphasized one theme—the importance of joy, proclaims that despite having just celebrated his ninetieth birthday, "Every day new hope keeps springing up in me. Isn't that miraculous at my age?"

*I*t was a warm and sunny California day when Jeannie Kimbrough decided to do a little grocery shopping and invited a friend to come along. She and her friend had returned to Jeannie's home and were putting away the groceries when Jeannie suddenly stopped dead in her tracks.

The voice was unmistakable to Jeannie: "Go check on your kids." She looked at her friend, but the woman was oblivious. There was no one else in the room. The voice came again: "Go check on your kids."

Jeannie's two-year-old daughter and three-year-old

son were playing outside. The neighborhood was safe and the kids well trained to stay out of the street, but Jeannie could not ignore the warning. A Christian who had been saved when she was thirteen, she knew immediately that it was God speaking to her.

Alice was hanging by her neck from the car window, which Jeannie had left open in the summer heat. Her brother, too small to know what to do or how to open the car door, was sitting in the car petrified.

"Oh my God," said Jeannie, and rushed to her daughter. A nurse, Jeannie could see that her daughter was alive at a glance, but she trembles to think what could have happened.

Then Alice started screaming at the top of her lungs, a sure sign that she was all right, and Jeannie helped her down.

It would have been ten or fifteen minutes before she'd checked on her kids if not for that mysterious voice. "If I hadn't paid attention to that voice, I would have had a dead baby," says Jeannie. "My daughter would have hung herself by then."

Neither of her kids, now grown and healthy, remember what had happened that day. But Jeannie believes the accident occurred when John decided to stand on one of his riding toys in order to crawl into the car through the half-open window. Alice tried to follow, and the toy she was standing on must have scooted out from under her feet. She was left hanging with her head in the car and her feet too short to reach the ground.

Jeannie professes that "the Lord had a reason for getting me outside the house. He was not ready to take my daughter." She says she also believes without a doubt that this was a true miracle that saved her daughter's life.

"God is real, does move, and cares about His children," she proclaims. "The Lord will take care of you and your family if you listen to Him. You have to listen to Him."

Spencer was a special cat from the beginning. He was born to a stray that Eileen Smith took in, and his mother died soon after his difficult birth. His cerebellum was damaged, which made him spastic, like a feline with cerebral palsy. He often fell.

"He probably should have been euthanized because he was so much trouble, but he was doing so well that I just took care of him," admits Eileen. She cared for Spencer for five months before he was able to stand up and manage by himself.

Spencer was a feisty little thing, although walking was

always difficult and he never lost the spastic movements.

The grayish-black kitten bonded to her from the beginning and Eileen returned Spencer's love and affection. He would cuddle up to her in bed every night and purr so loudly that she could feel the rumbling, lulling her to sleep.

One morning last year Eileen woke early, sensing that something was wrong. Spencer's soft melody had stopped. She reached out to him in the dark, and the small body was cool and still—even more alarming in the spastic little animal than it would be in a regular cat.

When Eileen examined the cat, a sense of shock swept over her. Spencer was dead. Although she is not a veterinarian, Eileen has worked as a registered nurse for more than three decades, and over the years she has operated both an animal rescue group and shelter. She has often seen people and animals die, and knows all the signs.

"As a nurse, I know reality. I know dead," she states unequivocally. "I've worked with dying patients and animals long enough. And, believe me, this animal was dead. I know what I saw."

There was nothing about Spencer to suggest life. There was no muscle tone, his eyes were lifeless, and his head was dangling, like a rag doll's.

Releasing her grip on the cat, Eileen began to cry.

"My heart broke," she says. Her own divorce was still a fresh wound. Her sister was seriously ill. And now this. She was overwhelmed. Spencer's loss was unbearable. He was the one presence in her life that could elicit a smile.

Eileen did what comes most naturally to her—she turned to prayer: "Please, God, not now!"

Eileen cradled Spencer in her arms and rocked him like a child. As the minutes ticked by, nothing had changed. There was no sign of life in him at all.

Twenty minutes had passed, and the grief-stricken pet owner was still watching her beloved cat.

And then, suddenly, she saw a twitch in his tail.

And then, little by little, small tremors shook Spencer. But his head was still listlessly hanging to the side.

Five minutes went by as Eileen watched the cat twitch more and more. And then, all of a sudden, Spencer's head snapped up. "It was like, 'Whoa, here I am.' I just can't explain it," says Eileen. Her cat had started purring again. He started, gently, affectionately, nipping at Eileen's face.

There were more tears, she recalls, but these were tears of joy. "I was so grateful—so overjoyed," she exclaims. "I just knew that my prayers had been answered. So many painful things had happened to me, but now I was given a gift. This cat was given back to me by God. It was nothing short of a miracle. . . ."

$\mathcal{P}$atricia A. Leone's friend Lorraine was diagnosed with lung cancer in 2002. "Lorraine was quite a phenomenal and spiritual woman and her life was all about contributing to others," Patricia says. "She did a lot of transformational work in people's lives and really believed in the magic of the universe. She was a very powerful and loving woman, and a big inspiration to me."

After the diagnosis, Lorraine's deteriorating health brought the two women closer than ever—it was a closeness shot with pain for Patricia, who had lost her mother to lung cancer as well. Lorraine had been a beautiful woman, but she was growing weaker and weaker, and her illness took away her good looks.

Lorraine's graciousness in death was an inspiration to Patricia. "Lorraine felt that she had completed her life and didn't struggle against the inevitable," Patricia says. Her friend opted to stop the chemotherapy treatments that would have prolonged her life, choosing instead to accept her eventual death.

On one particular August night, Patricia visited Lorraine in the hospital, bringing with her a healing candle she had made, wrapped in very cosmic-looking wrapping paper decorated with stars and the moon. Lorraine was surrounded by many people who loved her that night. She was bright and articulate, an inspiration to be with. She even had time to appreciate the wrapping paper, and Patricia tacked up a piece on the bulletin board in front of her. Patricia asked Lorraine if she could do a guided meditation with her that focused on healing. "No. Not yet," said Lorraine.

A week later, Lorraine still lingered. On Friday, Patricia determined she'd go over the next day. She thought it might be time for that guided meditation.

Throughout that Friday evening, Patricia could not get Lorraine out of her mind. "Something was calling to me, telling me not to delay much longer in seeing her," she says. That Saturday morning at about 6 A.M., Patricia jumped out of bed and literally raced over to the hospital. She could not explain how she knew it was urgent to get to Lorraine. Today, she believes God was speaking to her.

When she arrived, soon before eight o'clock, Patricia found that her friend had been moved to the hospital's hospice, where Lorraine was slipping in and out of consciousness. Lorraine was breathing heavily; Patricia could tell those breaths would be her last. Patricia sat down next to her.

She said, "Lorraine, remember I told you there was a meditation I wanted to do? It's time." She guided Lorraine into an alpha state and took her through a beautiful visualization—a light-filled forest, where Lorraine and Patricia were dancing together. She envisioned a white bridge that goes between this world and the next. She said, "Lorraine, on the other side of this bridge is everyone you ever loved—your parents and family are all waiting for you."

Although her dying friend was now in an unconscious state and could not respond, Patricia believes that Lorraine heard every word she said. We know that hearing is one of the last senses that leaves people.

Patricia took a little water and made the sign of the cross over Lorraine's head. Lorraine let out this long sigh of surrender and everything in the room became still.

Patricia put her head into Lorraine's lap and started crying. "I love you so much and I'll miss you so much," she said.

Several friends of Lorraine's joined Patricia, including a nun. They gathered around Lorraine and said a prayer. The moment they finished Lorraine passed away. At that moment Patricia experienced what she believes was a second miracle—one she proclaims she will remember for the rest of her life.

"It was like time had stopped for a moment," she recalls. "There was this energy in the room that I still can't adequately describe. It felt warm and it felt as if it were made of light. And this energy just moved right through my body from my head to my toes. My whole body flushed and started to tingle. I felt as if God had blessed me for being there and sent that blessing energy through me. I have never in my life experienced anything like that. It was like someone had waved a wand over me.

"I believe that I experienced two miracles," Patricia declares. "The miracle of God urging me over to the hospital just at the right time to facilitate Lorraine's passing to the other side, and then receiving a blessing from God for my efforts. It was really a phenomenal experience."

*L*os Angeles Police Department vice investigator Bill Rhetts was in a bad way on that warm Sunday afternoon in November. His personal life had fallen apart. He and his wife had separated, then divorced, soon after their two children were born. "I was very angry," he admits. "So I rebelled against God. I blamed Him for taking my family away."

A young Los Angeles police officer had plenty of opportunities to lose himself in wild activities. There were police groupies who followed cops around, and Bill started having sex with a lot of women. Every night he was out drinking—three six-packs a night. Alcohol had taken over his life. Sometimes he went to work drunk. Bill credits the grace of God for the fact that his career wasn't ruined.

Bill hit rock bottom—then began to heal. He knew he was not the man he should be. He began attending a nondenominational Christian church for the very first time, and, although he had been raised as a Catholic, he asked Jesus Christ to come into his life for the first time.

But his time on the wagon was short. He continued to sin. "There were spiritual conflicts trying to obey the Lord and walk with the Lord, versus the temptations on the job," he remembers. Bill adds that it became even more difficult to stay on the straight and narrow when he became an undercover cop with the vice squad that October.

Working vice meant being paid to drink on duty. A lot of investigative work involved being in bars and fraternizing with people who were involved with everything from gambling to prostitution. So there was more drinking going on in his life. And, then, after work, he often went out drinking with his friends.

Bill started dating several women, having shallow and temporary relationships. Bill says he was "hoping to find someone who would be a suitable companion for me." But, "my relationships were very shallow and temporary. When things began to go wrong, I would flee from the relationship. If I didn't flee, then they would flee. All of this compromising and hypocritical lifestyle were wrong choices. God was always speaking to me in the back of my mind. I knew what I was doing was wrong, but I didn't listen. I became a backsliding Christian. I had even stopped reading the Bible."

But something happened on a Sunday in November 1991 that turned Bill's life around. It wasn't like it was the first time he'd been in a shoot-out. He was no innocent, and had nearly been killed more than once. He had had to shoot men, sometimes fatally. But something different happened that day in a church parking lot.

That afternoon was beautiful, with blue skies and none of the usual smog hanging over the city of Los Angeles. Bill's partner was driving along a street in a primarily Hispanic neighborhood when Bill had what he describes as "a sixth sense." He told his partner to turn left. Five gang members were standing on the northwest corner of the intersection in front of a multistory brick church. "It's funny," Bill says, "but seeing that building reminded me that I should be in church on Sunday—not working the job."

Not minutes after he and his partner had first spotted the five men, there was a hail of gunfire. There were five suspects in an open area where there was no way to escape.

So Bill jumped out the right door, ran to the rear of the car, and lay down on the ground. Then he started to fire back, trying to give his partner cover so he could get out of the car. But his partner crawled into the back of the car with the police radio in his hand and hid there, leaving Bill, unaware that his partner hadn't tried to get out of the car, to defend himself alone.

Bill says no police cars arrived to help out, and the deadly gun battle continued. He could see that one guy in particular was doing most of the shooting, but all of the gang members were dressed in the same clothes, and sometimes Bill couldn't tell him from the others. "We were chasing each other around the cars like kids," Bill says, of their movements—but it was a serious game in which the players were trying to kill one another.

There were multiple bullet holes in Bill's car and other cars. There were bullet holes in the side of the church building that was right behind him. There was a moment when his enemy was no farther than six or eight feet away. The glass windows in the car Bill was crouched behind exploded all over the place, but Bill wasn't hit—by a bullet or even a shard of glass.

There was one moment when Bill ran out of ammunition and he thought his life was over. "The worst two sounds a police officer can hear is a click when you're expecting a bang—you're out of bullets—or a bang when you're expecting a click—an accidental discharge."

He heard the click when he was expecting a bang. He had to get another round of bullets out of the trunk of his car. And one guy was still shooting at him. He was screaming, "Lord, Lord, help me, help me," and screaming to his partner. When there was no response, he began to suspect his partner had been shot and killed.

Bill managed to reload his weapon. Then he got a good view of the gang member who was shooting at him. He remembers lining up his target in his gun sight and, as he did so, also thinking about God.

"I told the Lord, 'If you save me through this shooting—because I want to go home and see my girls when I visit them—I will recommit my life to you.'" Bill squeezed the trigger, fired off a couple of rounds, and fatally wounded the shooter. "I will never forget that last squeeze. It was a perfect middle of the head shot and he went down."

As the other gang members fled, Bill remembers cautiously approaching the dying gunman. "As the deceased lay on the ground, I noticed a pool of blood. Within a few minutes his blood had surrounded him. What immediately came to mind was the Precious Blood of Jesus. It was at that very moment that I began to mourn the sins I had committed during my backsliding days. I then renewed my commitment to the Lord."

At 12:01 in the afternoon, in a church parking lot while the church services were going on, the Lord had brought a backsliding Christian back to where he should have been. Bill's partner didn't help him, the dispatcher couldn't help him, the backup was too late, and Bill admits that his tactics were nothing special. Only the Lord had helped him. "I should've been dead, but the Lord was shielding me with His armor," says Bill.

Bill doesn't think it was any coincidence that this all took place just outside of a church. "There was a message there for me. And I believe it was a miracle that I ran out of ammunition and still had time to reload without being killed." He also considers it a miracle that despite the confusion at times involved in trying to identify who the shooter was among the gang members, he was able to identify and then kill his attacker.

Later in the day, Bill learned that the gang members were waiting in the parking lot to kill members of a rival gang who had recently accepted God and were inside the church attending a discipleship class. "It's awesome to see how God provided protection for *all* His children," he avows. "Only God knows what innocent blood might have been shed in the church if some instinct hadn't told me to drive by there."

Since the day of that shooting, Bill has been a committed Christian. "That was God's wake-up call for me and I've kept my commitment to the Lord," he declares. "I got married and cleaned up my R-rated lifestyle. I've stayed in fellowship with other believers. I share my faith and my testimony, and do my best not to compromise my walk with Him."

*J*ane Mullikin wasn't a stranger to the notion that an unseen presence could guide and inform her.

The first time the Florida resident knew something mysterious was looking out for her was when her mother died suddenly when she was twenty-five, and she realized that she had been preparing for that moment and mourning for three months before it happened. A feeling of homesickness had come over her suddenly one day, only to be understood when her father called and told her what she already knew—that her mother had died.

The second time was when Jane was thirty, and her doctor told her she was expecting her third child. The child was unplanned, and as she drove home, she wondered if she should have an abortion. All of a sudden, as she passed over the Wabash River, in southern Illinois, it seemed that a small fluffy cloud was surrounding her and following her car.

A warm feeling engulfed Jane and she heard a voice saying, "Everything is okay. Everything is okay." When she got home, Jane told her husband she was pregnant and she was going to have the baby.

Her baby was three months old the third time she knew God had intervened in her life. That miracle took place in her life in 1971 when Jane went for a medical examination and the doctors let her know she had bone cancer. In 1971 bone cancer was a killer, and a fast one.

Jane decided to forego treatment and to enjoy her baby for however long she had to live instead of having surgery. But nothing happened. "Either I didn't have bone cancer or *somebody* took it away," she says.

The fourth time that Jane experienced what she describes as God's physical presence was years later. Her second marriage had broken up, badly, and she was packing to move to Florida. Jane was alone in the house when she felt a presence, as if somebody were standing right beside her.

"But I couldn't see anybody. And all of a sudden, just like that first time in my car, a cloud surrounded me. I could feel it and I could see it. It was a warm, loving, safe, and secure feeling like I was being held in someone's arms. And, once again, the message was, 'Everything will be okay.' I didn't hear it with my ears; I heard it with my spirit. It was another miracle. I was being reassured at a time when my life was in disarray."

Jane regrets the fact that she didn't credit God for any of these incidents. "Here I was developing a pattern of God miraculously intervening in my life, but I didn't acknowledge it. In fact, after I survived bone cancer I became much more selfish. I became more involved with the idea of what do I want out of life instead of thinking about the Lord. This kind of thinking took me on a path that led me further and further from God."

It took two and a half years from the fourth time she was aware of God's presence for Jane to realize what all this meant. She lived as a semi-recluse, mostly financially supported by her now-grown children. It was at the end of that long period of withdrawal and reflection, a time when Jane says she did much thinking about how God had miraculously appeared in her life, that she made a conscious decision to move closer to the Lord. She decided to go to work, put food on her table, and spend much of her time getting reacquainted with God. Jane strove to be one of God's more loyal servants, and God made His presence known again.

It all began at a religious service she attended several months ago, a prayer group for a family in need of help. A hot coal-like feeling began to pulse through her whole body, painfully. It was hot and it hurt. But Jane wasn't thinking about herself. She was thinking about the others and the words of the prayer. "Yet it was happening to me," she says. All day she had felt like she was getting a cold, but it never materialized.

Intrigued by what she had experienced, Jane began to watch a television program featuring Lindsay and Richard Roberts, televangelists from Oral Roberts University who said that faith in God was the key to healing. She believed that. After a while, Jane began to raise her hand when instructed by them, and she prayed for the healing of her spirit night after night.

Jane had had a hard, goose egg–size lump under her arm for thirty-four years. It was painful, and every doctor she'd gone to was certain it was cancerous, but Jane refused a biopsy. The second time she watched Lindsay and Richard Roberts's show, it suddenly dawned on her that the lump hadn't bothered her recently.

She reached under her arm and could not find it. The fatty tissue was still there, but it was soft.

"It was God who was working on not only healing

my spirit, but my body as well," she joyfully proclaims. "Now I go to be tested every year, and my last mammogram showed that lump to be gone. I don't think my doctor believed anything I told him about having had a faith healing—but I certainly did!"

Since that day, Jane attests that she has been healed of other serious illnesses as well—everything from arthritis to bursitis—and that she no longer uses the sinus medication she had used for years. She emphasizes that such healings are the result of prayer and faith.

"Since I found God, I'm in the best physical shape that I've ever been in," she gratefully declares at sixty-one. "Miracles have become part of my everyday life—part of my all-the-time existence."

$\mathcal{K}$ay Parks was a sophomore at Redwood Junior Academy in Santa Rosa, California, excitedly making plans to attend a Seventh-day Adventist boarding school. Along with the paperwork, there was a requirement that she get a physical exam.

The teenager expected to pass her physical with flying colors—after all, she was young and in perfect health. But the doctor heard a heart murmur. He sent her to a lab for blood tests. The next day, Kay received a call to return to her doctor's office.

The blood tests indicated rheumatic fever, and that was probably the cause of the heart murmur. He said she'd have to take it easy. Boarding school was out of the question. Kay would have to stay in bed for about a year. "Maybe after a year in bed I'll allow you to go to public school," he told her.

Kay was heartbroken. She said, "This can't really be happening." She was too shocked to do anything, but her mother called her grandmother with the news. Kay's grandmother was a woman of unbreakable faith and there was no doubt in her mind that God heals.

She called the pastor of the church where she and Kay were regular attendees. Although Kay's mother was a sporadic churchgoer and her father almost never attended, Kay's grandmother's faith and prayer had always been an inspiration and a model to Kay. The pastor came over for prayer and anointing. Then Kay's grandmother contacted the elders of the church and some other church members and they also came over to the house to pray over Kay. "I was on everyone's prayer list," says Kay.

Kay submits that the first effect of the prayers was that they made her feel grateful. But she didn't feel anything. A believer since she was a child, she knew that God listens to prayers, but she didn't know exactly how it was going to work out. Still, she had faith that she would be healed enough so that she could go away to school, as she had dreamed.

So Kay was much less baffled than her doctor when she returned to his office for a follow-up appointment a few weeks after the initial diagnosis. He checked her and rechecked her and rechecked her and there was no indication of a heart murmur. Kay told him about the prayer sessions, and he said, "No, no, no." He sent her back to the lab for more blood work.

The laboratory results showed no trace of any disease. There was no sign of anything ever having been wrong with her. There was no heart murmur and there was nothing to show that she had had rheumatic fever. "It really was a miracle. It was the day that God healed my heart," Kay says.

Whenever Kay goes for a physical examination, she mentions once having been diagnosed with a heart murmur. Her doctors have always checked and, more than thirty years later, there's never been anything there.

The following school year, Kay was attending Lodi Academy exactly according to plan. Her grandmother was the proudest. "She told the church members that their prayers had been answered and that God had healed me."

Kay pauses and adds an afterthought. "As remarkable as this event was, it was not a grand finale of how

God showed me His power and His love for me. It was only the beginning. I don't know why, but I do know that the Lord has saved my life on many occasions." She adds that these testimonies "could fill up an entire book. This miracle was a life-changing experience and it was the start of what has been for me an amazing relationship with God."

Kay says it all boils down to how the power of prayer can bring about healing and other miracles. "Prayer is a means for people to grow stronger with the Lord, and that's why He answers," she declares. "Earnest prayers are the key because they increase a person's faith and make you grow stronger in your walk with God."

The oldest of four children, Dale Marie spent much of her childhood moving from state to state because her father was a career U.S. Army officer. A strict disciplinarian, her father was often cruel to her. "He ran our household like a sergeant, and that included a lot of undue punishment to us kids," she describes.

Dale began feeling depressed at age seventeen. "I guess it started with my background with my father— with him being abusive—and feeling dislocated from my family," she explains. Her life became an ongoing struggle with depression.

As the years passed she eventually got hooked on prescription drugs. "I would make up illnesses at the doctor's office just to get all kinds of prescription drugs," she relates. "I would make up stories that I had back problems and this and that just to get painkillers. These drugs would help me kill the mental pain I was feeling."

It grew harder and harder for Dale to continue living. Her life had become a constant struggle. Her family always looked down on mental illness, which made it harder to get help. She feared that if they found out about her depression, they would shun her altogether. Dale hid her mental problems from everyone but her husband, Warren.

Dale's condition was worsening. She started to take more pills, trying to dull her anguish. She took more and more at a time, hoping she would kill herself. "I would try to kill myself, wake up, and be angry that I was still alive. So I'd try to kill myself again." Suicide filled her thoughts.

She took as many as 150 aspirin at a time, and as many as 50 prescription pills, but she still woke up the next morning.

Things began to shift for Dale when she accepted a chance invitation to church. Her children were in a

Baptist Bible school, and one day she was invited to come. It was on a Sunday, and that day she gave her life to Christ.

Dale hoped this would mark the end of her self-destructive behavior, but it did not. "I felt that I had been saved, but I still wasn't very much into religion," she explains. "I just kind of dabbled with it." She attended that Baptist church for a while, but it didn't stick.

Her prescription drug habit continued. Her husband left her, and she and her two children moved in with her sister, who had just split with her own husband, who had been an alcoholic. The living arrangement didn't last. "She basically kicked me out," says Dale.

Dale believes that all this pressure sent her on a particularly bad drug bender. Her depression deepened. She and her kids moved in with her brother.

Dale ingested a large number of prescription drugs in another attempt to kill herself. But she caught sight of her children and said to herself, "My God, what am I doing?" She drove herself to the Walter Reed mental hospital. She told them what she had done and she was hospitalized.

Dale spent two weeks at the hospital. Upon her release she made a promise to herself to try to change her life. She went back to New York where her husband, who was in the Coast Guard at the time, was living. She moved into a town house located near his base. A neighbor invited her to her church.

At the neighbor's church Dale found a very different kind of service from those she had experienced before. A nondenominational church, it felt very spiritual to her. She felt connected for the first time in her life. "The teachings were great," she says. "I felt I was now where I was supposed to be with the Lord." Dale started reading the Bible.

The good times didn't last. Dale suffered another set-back. One morning when she was feeling depressed again, she thought, "I just can't take this anymore—I just can't." She had been given Prozac when she got out of the hospital, and had been warned that if she took too many of these she would die.

Dale remembers stepping into the shower that morning with thoughts of ending her life once and for all. She had reached her rope's end. "Then I decided I was going to make one last attempt at calling out to God and have Him help me. I stood in the shower and I was calling His name out loud and pleading for Him to help me. I held my hands up in the air and I was worshiping the Lord, shouting out His name."

As she stood in the shower Dale felt something touch the top of her head and move over her entire body to her toes. It was like somebody had washed every bit of depression out of her body and the sun had just come out. She knew at that moment that her prayers had been answered and that she was healed.

Stepping out of the shower, Dale heard the neighbor who had asked her to come to church knocking on her door. "Oh, my goodness, I can see it on your face," said the woman.

"I don't need my medication anymore. I'm not depressed." Dale was skipping through the house and hopping up and down like a kid. She had never felt that good before. "It was a release from everything. For two hours that day I felt the Lord's presence all around me."

Since that miraculous moment in her shower, four years have passed. Dale has never taken another Prozac—not even in the prescribed dose. She has not experienced any further bouts of depression. "I'm free of depression that plagued my life for nearly twenty years," she joyously proclaims. "I will say without any doubt that what happened to me was a miracle. Part of that miracle is that my husband and I got together again. He recognized a tremendous change in me—that I was now a happy person."

Dale is now devoted to the religious life. "I became a new Christian after that experience. I read Scripture and sometimes I can sit for hours reading through the Bible. I go to the Marketplace Church twice a week and I often share my testimony with the congregation."

Sharing her story is important to Dale. "I know there's a lot of people out there going through the same thing that I went through," she explains, "and I try to give them hope. I tell people that my life was saved and I can't ever think of being without the Lord in my life. I would die without Him. I also tell them that our Heavenly Father does want to heal us from our pain and that He is, indeed, a worker of miracles."

*R*ita Kurgan, a Philadelphia schoolteacher and professional intuitive is seated at her booth at a New Age Expo recently held at a New York City convention center. The attractive psychic is asking people who come by her booth to hand her a favorite item so that she can get impressions from it and give a reading. Customers walk away from their session looking pleased at what they have just heard.

Rita became involved with her intuitive practice as a result of a miraculous healing she received involving a painful and chronic jaw condition. She is thinking about leaving her position teaching in a high school to devote herself full-time to helping others through her intuitive skills.

Rita takes some time out between clients to relate a story about her long and winding road that led from a lukewarm connection to God to a miracle that she avows healed her severe jaw and face pain—a healing that renewed her faith in God.

Rita developed temporomandibular joint syndrome, commonly known as TMJ, a dental disorder that occurs when one's jaw is misaligned, as a child. This condition can lead to a host of physical problems, including severe neck and back pain.

One day in the mid-1990s Rita overexerted herself in the course of a move and the pain that was always with her got worse. She went to see a chiropractor who administered a traction-type of treatment, which only intensified her pain.

For four years Rita's jaw was in terrible and constant pain after she saw the chiropractor. She visited various doctors and dentists—both conventional and alternative practitioners—in an effort to alleviate the pain. She attempted suicide more than once. "I sometimes refer to myself as 'the suicide that lived,'" she admits.

But something else was happening, too. As Rita went

from doctor to doctor, she found herself praying to God for relief.

Rita had to take an extended sick leave from her job. "I had chiropractors inserting all kinds of different appliances in my mouth to try to treat the TMJ problem," she says. "It was a mess, uncomfortable, and nothing worked."

In 1988, feeling desperate about her physical condition, Rita contacted a spiritual healer from Canada. She started reading inspirational literature and listening to healing tapes. It was her formal introduction to the idea of spiritual healing.

From this point forward, Rita started noticing strange coincidences that whispered of something more in life.

For example, she was looking out the window of her apartment one day and she saw a truck passing by with the letters *G.O.D.* emblazoned on its side. "Sure, the letters stood for "Guaranteed Overnight Delivery—but did they really?"

Turning away from the window, Rita switched on her radio and the song that was playing was "I'll Be There," by the Four Tops. Was there a connection between the letters on the truck and the song on the radio?

Rita says that as these strange coincidences continued, she began to think that they were more than just coincidences. She started to believe that God was guiding her and giving her puzzle pieces to put together. "For the first time in my life, I really became aware that something else was going on in the universe that I had for too long ignored."

Eventually, Rita reached the conclusion that "when we pray to God and we talk to God, He answers us in coincidences. God can't actually talk to us, but if we pay attention, He guides us to do certain things at certain times."

With this in mind, Rita says she began praying fervently to God to guide her to the right practitioner who would eliminate her jaw pain. "I was praying for a miracle," she submits, "and I believe I got one."

This type of behavior was completely new to Rita. She had grown up in a Jewish household where religion played little part in her family's daily life. Her family went to synagogue on the High Holy Days, Rosh Hashanah and Yom Kippur, "but religion wasn't much of a big deal to me," she says.

Throughout high school and college, Rita was estranged from organized religion. "I always felt like a spiritual person and I always had an idea that there was something out there, but I never believed in what the religious organizational structures had to say."

But here she was praying to God to help relieve her pain. A few weeks later Rita visited a chiropractor whom she believes she was guided to by God. "I was at my wit's end," she recalls. She was out of money and energy. Chiropractors and dentists were now refusing to accept her as a patient; they said nothing more could be done for her.

One night, in pain and depression, Rita cried out to God: "I will accept what you want for me. If you want me to get better, fine. If you don't, I'll try to live with the pain or whatever because I can't go searching anymore. This is it. I surrender to You." Rita knew this was the end of the road.

Rita's first miracle was finding a chiropractor who would accept her as his patient, even though he knew about her history of failed treatment. He gave her a chiropractic mouth device that is manufactured in Australia and that is designed to align the jaw. Rita's pain lessened immediately.

He also referred her to another chiropractor named Dr. John Finnitt, who used a system called neuroemotional technique, a form of energy healing focused on the premise that negative emotions contribute to pain.

Rita had been experiencing tremendous emotional pain about a miscarriage she had had. Dealing with that issue made her feel much better.

A year after that plea in the night, when she surrendered herself to God's will, Rita's pain had completely disappeared. She is convinced that her prayers were answered. "I *absolutely* believe He guided me to the right doctor once I asked for His help," she declares with conviction. "I *absolutely* believe that. I can't define God for you, but based upon my own experience I certainly know that He exists."

Rita is in constant communication with the Creator now. She has devoted her life to helping others, sharing her own experience. She recognizes her own talent and believes she was meant for this work.

Rita has a single piece of advice for anyone who is suffering from physical pain, and that is to keep believing that they can be healed. "There is always Highest Good and grace," she declares. "If you believe in God and the possibilities of your getting well, you can manifest healing. Just accept that there's a reason for what you're going through, and that God has a plan for you."

*K*elly Franklin says it's a miracle that she was even born. Her father was a violent man who once beat his wife so severely while she was pregnant that the baby died and Kelly's mother suffered a ruptured uterus.

Because of all the scarring and damage, the doctors told Kelly's mother that she would never conceive again. However, within a few years she was again pregnant — this time with Kelly. Kelly was almost full term when her father beat her mother again. For the second time, Kelly's mother was rushed to surgery.

The doctors expected Kelly to die. She was born by cesarean section—bumped and bruised from her father's brutality, and with a concussion.

The doctors thought it was a miracle birth. They called Kelly their "angel child." Kelly's aunt still calls her "angel baby." When Kelly's mother conceived again, her son was born dead.

But the life Kelly survived to lead was a difficult one. Her father was an electronic genius who worked for the phone company when her parents were married. They lived in Temple, Texas, and were pretty well off. They had a house, a boat, and a couple of cars. But Kelly's father was always getting drunk and beating up her mother. Kelly's mother would run to her own mother, and then come back.

Kelly's mother finally left her father when Kelly was small. She took out a restraining order against Kelly's father, and he had no visiting rights. But Kelly's mother would allow him to take her over the weekends. "I don't know why she did these things after the way he treated her," says Kelly.

Kelly was five years old when her father kidnapped her—he picked her up at school on Friday, and from there drove straight to Canada from Texas. At first, Kelly's father was able to hold a job and make money. She didn't want for a lot in terms of a material things.

But she was left alone a lot while her father worked. "I was in the first grade and really raising myself," she says.

But the worst was yet to come.

Her father's drinking got worse. He began to lose jobs and there was no money. They moved frequently; Kelly went to a dozen or more schools in a year, never learning anything.

Then the physical abuse began. Kelly was raped and beaten. Her father would shoot at her and throw knives at her. Sometimes he left her for days without food. There are incidents Kelly still can't even talk about; her husband doesn't even know everything that happened to her.

Through all of this, Kelly was deeply religious. Kelly's mother was Catholic and her father Baptist, but neither was a faithful churchgoer. Every once in a while, her father would have an attack of conscience and take Kelly to an Assembly of God church. But her faith was her own.

She recalls this incident from before she was taken from her mother: she was watching the sunset and her mother said, "Kelly, what are you doing?"

The little girl said, "I'm watching the sun come down."

"Why?" asked her mother.

"Because I see Jesus coming down with it," said Kelly.

Kelly was eleven when her faith was rewarded. She

was living with her father in a shack in Robertson, Texas, that didn't even have a bathroom or hot running water. Her father had just forced her to have sex with him.

Kelly ran out of the cabin without any clothes on. She fell down on her knees, and cried out to God, "Why, why, why is this happening to me? I can't take it anymore. Please save me."

It was a few days later, and Kelly was washing dishes. Her father hadn't been home for two or three days. All of a sudden she sensed a woman standing behind her.

Kelly turned. There was no one there. But she thought she could smell perfume. But it dawned on her that it wasn't perfume—it was flowers: roses and lilies. The smell was almost overwhelming, as if it were inside her nose.

There was also something in the air. It was like electricity dancing on her skin. And there was a wind that felt like it was blowing right through her. Her fear was gone, and she was filled with peace.

Later that afternoon, Kelly's father returned home. They were sitting there, watching television, and he was drinking. He said, "Come here and take your clothes off." She said, "No!"

He got up to hit her, and just at that moment the attic door flew off its hinges. A huge wind whipped through the house and, again, Kelly smelled roses and lilies. It was like a gale-force wind and the windows of the shack started vibrating and raising and falling. The most amazing thing of all was that this was a hot, smoldering Texas summer day with no wind outside.

Kelly's hair was blowing, but the place where she was standing was the eye of the storm. Blowing all around her was wind. Then she looked into her father's eyes and she saw something that she had never seen there before—fear and confusion. He said, "I didn't want to have sex, anyway," and he walked out.

Kelly sat there with the wind still blowing around her for a few more minutes, wondering what had just happened. Was it a ghost, protecting her? She said to herself, "I'm not even going to ask. I'm just going to sit here and watch TV and thank God that whatever happened, happened."

Whatever happened, it continued to happen every time her father threatened her. Six or seven times, he was prevented by what seemed to be a paranormal disturbance, always beginning with a wind blowing through their cabin. Once a fan broke with a loud noise. Another time, one fell on him when he was trying to force himself on her. Every time, Kelly's father left her alone in the cabin.

From that time on, Kelly became a big believer in

miracles. "I could understand a miracle happening one time—but six or seven? All I could think is that God had answered my prayers and now I had a protector in my life."

Although she continued to live in fear of her father, he no longer abused her, though he continued to drink heavily. Kelly finally escaped and returned to her mother who was living in Mexico at the time. She grew up, married, and established a happy home with her husband and two children.

"This gift that was given to me from God—maybe She was a spirit, maybe She was an angel, or maybe it was Mary. I just don't know. I just know it was a miracle. I never saw her, although this was not the last time that She has appeared in my life. I still get that scent of roses and lilies at times when I need help."

For anyone experiencing the kind of abuse she did when she was younger, Kelly has this piece of advice to offer: "Never give up hope and never give up on yourself because God can create miracles. What you are going through can be a lesson so that you will be able to someday help others like I'm trying to do by telling people my story."

*G*iven the extent of the injuries that she suffered in her automobile acci- dent, Kailyn Daniels shouldn't be alive today — let alone able to walk across a room by herself or consume food without use of a feeding tube. If not dead, she should be paralyzed or severely brain damaged. Miraculously, less than two months after her near-fatal traffic accident dis- located her head from her spine, the twenty-one-year-old senior at Warner Pacific College in Portland, Oregon, was walking, talking, and doing just fine.

Kailyn's ordeal and miraculous recovery began about

8:30 P.M. on Tuesday, September 25, 2001. After a long afternoon of school and teaching piano, she was heading home on South Beavercreek Road. Just minutes from her home, she was crossing an intersection when her navy blue Ford Escort was broadsided on the driver's side by a sixteen-year-old girl who ran the stop sign at about seventy miles per hour. The last thing Kailyn can remember is seeing the Beaver Creek Fire Department.

She nearly died in the wreckage of that car accident. Her driver's door was sheared off from the impact, the roof was ripped open, the axles on all the wheels had been destroyed, and the driver's seat was found resting in the passenger's seat. Neighbors later said the crash sounded like a bomb exploding. The Escort was sent spinning, finally coming to rest in the front yard of a nearby house. Although the sixteen-year-old driver of the other car and her passenger escaped unhurt, Kailyn was not so fortunate.

Beaver Creek is a very small town, and the fire department doesn't always have a paramedic on duty. But on Tuesday nights at around 8:30 the department holds paramedic drills, so help came much more quickly than it might have. When the paramedics arrived at the rural crossroads that night, they found Kailyn unconscious and barely breathing. Her liver had been badly lacerated, the internal bleeding was massive, and her head had been nearly severed. When she arrived at the Oregon Health Sciences University Trauma Center, twenty-six minutes away, doctors predicted she would either die in the next few hours or be paralyzed from the head down.

Kailyn underwent immediate surgery to repair her damaged liver. Doctors wouldn't realize for another three days that the force of the impact had literally separated her skull from her spinal column. Had Kailyn been awake and moved the injured neck, she could have done even more damage to her body.

Kailyn had already been in surgery for several hours by the time her family got to the hospital. Doctors told her parents, Kermit and Carol, that Kailyn's neck was broken, and that it pretty much looked like she had brain damage. If she survived at all, she would probably end up being a quadriplegic or paraplegic. They also told Kermit and Carol about the large number of infections that were attacking the young woman's broken body.

At one point during the night-long surgery, Kailyn went into cardiac arrest. Dr. John Mayberry, the hospital's trauma surgeon, opened her chest and massaged her heart by hand until it started beating again. Dr. Mayberry feared she wouldn't make it through this procedure—it was a last resort and not many patients recover. He said he was just about ready to give up when her heart started beating again. A believer himself, Dr. Mayberry has declared Kailyn's survival of the surgery a miracle.

Three weeks later, she was still in a coma in the intensive care trauma unit and holding on for dear life. Kailyn's memories are very cloudy until the time when surgery began to reattach her neck. She woke up soon after that, having no idea how badly she had been injured. She also didn't know that a prayer network was stretching around the world via the Internet.

Kailyn's doctors decided it was all right for her to return home less than a week after she regained consciousness. Reflecting back, Kailyn proclaims that her deep and abiding faith in God is what brought her through this ordeal. "Faith is the strongest thing that you can have," she declares. "I was touched by the hand of God and I'm grateful to be alive. I'm grateful for the smallest things like being able to tie my shoelaces. He gave me the strength and the courage to get through all of this."

Kailyn says she is still going through a recovery period. She has undergone several subsequent surgeries. She suffers mostly from hip pain, which doctors hope to correct soon. Her biggest concern, however, is paying her massive medical bills, which are quickly approaching

$600,000. Nonetheless, she is convinced that God will also remedy that situation.

What's next for this miracle girl? "I've been very, very blessed and I want to give back," she says. "One of the things I want to do is work with troubled teens. I want to be an inspiration to others the way everyone has been to me. I want to tell them and anyone else I can that if such a miracle can happen to me it can happen to anyone."

Kailyn says there is one more interesting footnote to her story. "You know, after the collision all my college books in the trunk were muddy, torn, and wrecked. Even my CD player in the trunk had to be pried open, and the CDs inside were broken from the force of the crash. But my Bible was in perfect condition. It only had some glass covering it in one spot. Can you imagine? Talk about God stating right then and there that His Word lasts forever."

$\mathcal{I}$f you met Basil Hoffman nine years ago and tried to talk to him about God, he would have politely changed the subject or, worse, made a derogatory comment about religion. That's because for most of his adult life he had been an atheist, although he received some religious training as a child.

Today that no longer is the case. The Glendale, California, resident says his dramatic change of mind came on the very same evening that he experienced a miracle.

Basil grew up in the Jewish faith. He went to

Sunday school and Hebrew school, and was even bar mitzvahed at thirteen and confirmed at age sixteen.

But Basil moved away from the Lord. He never acquired a workable concept of God as an ever-present source of life; God was never real to him. By the time Basil was in college, he was avoiding all religious activities. And by his graduation he was an atheist.

"I was convinced that God was silly and a contrivance, just as most atheists believe," he says now. "If the question ever came up about 'aren't you interested? Don't you want to inquire about the universe, blah, blah, blah?' I would have said, 'No, and why should I?' I grew up regarding man and the universe as rationally unexplainable."

Basil's health problem was the key to his change of heart. It began soon after his graduation from college — a temporary but recurring pain and loss of strength in his right hand that showed itself when he lifted weights. At first, he ignored it. It always went away after a few minutes, and he figured it was nothing.

But then Basil met his future wife, Christine. As fate would have it, Christine was Basil's spiritual opposite — she was a devout Christian Scientist and had already been studying Christian Science for ten years when they got married.

Christine's conversion to Christian Science had come

after a healing she experienced, but she had regarded herself as a spiritual person all her life. She believed very much in God and had studied various religious and meta-physical things.

Despite the religious differences between Christine and Basil, the marriage was happy. "We were tolerant of each other," says Basil, although he acknowledges that it had to be "on some level" painful for Christine to know that not only did he not share any of her beliefs, but to some extent he looked down on them.

As Basil grew older, the condition in his right arm got worse. He was in his thirties when writing with his right hand, his dominant hand, became painful. He was forced to teach himself to write with his left hand instead.

Then Basil noticed something new—a tremor had developed. Now Basil was afraid, because he had close relatives who had been affected by tremors that progressed to worsening debilitation for at least two generations.

The tremor got worse and worse, and Basil tried to ignore it. At first he associated it with lifting weights. Later on he attributed it to not sleeping enough or to a little bit of stress or drinking too much coffee.

Basil had become functionally left-handed, not using his right hand at all, when he met an orthopedic surgeon at a dinner party he attended with his wife. In the course of dinner conversation, he mentioned that he hadn't always been a lefty. His host, a renowned neurosurgeon, said he had a colleague coming to the dinner who was an orthopedic surgeon with a considerable background in problems like Basil's.

The orthopedic surgeon gave Basil a business card and an invitation to drop by his office for a consultation. The doctor had a diagnosis: focal action dystonia.

He gave Basil exercises to do, but they did little. There was an expensive drug that the doctor thought might help, but Basil found it completely ineffective.

By now, Basil had devised creative ways of hiding his right hand. He was even trying to hide the extent of his problem from his wife. One night, Basil couldn't get the key in the lock of his house because his hand was shaking so much. This grip—the same required to hold a pen—was particularly difficult.

Christine was right behind him and she saw the whole thing. It was the final straw. "You really have to deal with this problem," she said. Basil tried humor: "I have dealt with it. I'm left-handed." But Christine wanted Basil to go to a Christian Scientist practitioner.

Basil hedged. For years he had avoided anything having to do with religion, and he certainly didn't want to start getting involved at this point. Christine pleaded with her husband. Basil finally went just to make his wife happy.

When Basil arrived at the Christian Scientist practitioner's apartment in Hollywood, he thought he was entering the Twilight Zone—that it was all ridiculous. "I really didn't expect anything positive to come out of it. I thought I would go in, be subjected to who knows what, pay her the twenty bucks, and be gone."

Basil recalls that a "little redheaded lady" answered the door and invited him to come inside. The healer talked to him for a few minutes about the hand, and she began to do something strange—some of the time she was speaking to Basil and it seemed that some of the time she was speaking to God. Basil had no frame of reference for what was going on, and most of what she said meant absolutely nothing to him.

The session lasted no longer than fifteen to twenty minutes—maybe even less. Then the healer said, "Would you like to write something?"

Basil smiled politely. "Sure."

She placed a pen and writing pad on the table. Basil started writing with his right hand and he wrote . . . and wrote . . . and wrote. There was no pain, no difficulty grasping the pen, no shaking. Only writing.

To this very day, Basil shakes his head in wonderment when he recalls that evening. "In less than twenty minutes I was permanently healed of a disability that had been with me for most of my adult life. The most remarkable aspect of the healing was that my atheism didn't prevent it."

Basil looked up in amazement at the practitioner; all he saw was an expression of certainty on her face. There was no question in her mind about what had just happened. Her incredulous patient said, "I need to know more about this." She was matter-of-fact: She just accepted the healing. Such things were obviously a part of her everyday life.

Over the years, Basil has replayed the events of that evening over and over again in his mind. He has come to believe that the practitioner's faith was greater than his skepticism and his belief that he had a problem. "I had walked in there thinking that something was wrong with me—she knew that there wasn't."

Basil continues to visit the practitioner's home. He has become a believer. He regularly studies the Bible as well as Christian Science literature, as a way to demonstrate his gratitude to God for his healing.

"My health is better than ever, my finances are better, my career is better—it's just amazing what God can do," he joyfully proclaims. "I am grateful beyond words to God. I could never go back to being an atheist. It's even hard for me to remember where I was before this happened to me and how I could even have been that person—I'm so different now."

*D*ebbie Renninger was eighteen years old and she needed to have some wisdom teeth extracted. But before any anesthetic could be administered, the dentist asked her to get a chest x-ray to make certain she didn't have anything wrong that could complicate the treatment.

When Debbie's doctor studied the x-ray, he did not like what he saw. He sent Debbie to a Pittsburgh hospital to see a cancer specialist for further testing. His suspicions were confirmed by all the more sophisticated tests: Debbie had Hodgkin's disease. Debbie had to remain in the hospital and she was scheduled for a biopsy in three days.

Debbie remembers that when she heard the news she couldn't believe it. She told her parents that she didn't have any disease, much less a serious one. She was just out of high school and starting her life. Her skepticism was validated by one thing: She was completely asymptomatic. Debbie couldn't believe God would take her life at that juncture.

Debbie was raised in a religious household, and she immediately turned to prayer. She sought help from her minister. She remembers on the day that she entered the hospital she sat in her room and thought that God would heal anything the doctors found.

Debbie's religious Methodist parents had taught her that there was something greater than doctors. They always felt that if you went for surgery or something, there was a greater hand guiding the surgeon's hand. God had the final say when it came to healing, Debbie had always believed.

On the day before her surgery was scheduled, Bill Morgan, pastor of Connellsville's Wesley Church, arrived in Debbie's hospital room. After an hour's visit, he said to her, "Debbie, I'm going to say a prayer for you." He took her hands in both of his and started praying.

Debbie will never forget that moment—one in which she believes something extraordinary happened to her; something which she can only describe as a miracle. She felt a hand on her head. The minister's hands were still holding hers, so she knew the hand wasn't his. A warm sensation went through her body and she felt as if something were being lifted out of her.

Debbie's first reaction was confusion, followed by a strong feeling that God was touching her.

Debbie went through the biopsy procedure with great peace of mind. The biopsy was performed and it came back negative. Nothing was wrong with her at all. She was overjoyed.

"I just couldn't stop thanking God for saving my life. When I told my parents what had happened, they rejoiced and started to cry. They told the minister and he told different people in the church and everyone praised God for my healing."

Six weeks later, Debbie returned to her doctor for a follow-up visit. "I would have bet a year's salary that your daughter had Hodgkin's disease," he told her parents. When Debbie and her folks described the miraculous occurrence that took place in her hospital room, "he just looked at us like we were whacko and didn't say a word," as Debbie describes it.

To this day, Debbie is firmly convinced she was the

recipient of a miracle. "I had a faith healing and nobody can ever take this belief from me," she declares. "I know for sure that miracles are out there. I don't know why I was chosen for a miracle. I just believe that He has a plan for me. I still don't know what that plan is. All I do know for sure is that God healed me."

For anyone diagnosed with a serious disease, Debbie suggests that they trust in God. "Pray, because there's great power in prayer," she proclaims. "And you must also have faith. I had the faith that I didn't have this disease and I believed that God didn't want me to have this disease because I was just starting my life. And God heard me."

*W*henever she walks past Ground Zero, the site of the former World Trade Center, Alpha—her spiritual name—is grateful that she was not among those who perished there. If not for a miraculous transformation in her life about a year before the tragedy, she would have been at work on the very floor that was directly struck by an airplane on September 11.

Alpha, who was born in Tajikistan in Central Asia and raised in Israel and Austria before coming here with her family, says as a Jew from a mostly Muslim country, she did not receive much exposure to religion as a young child. "We went to synagogue, but not all the time — mostly on the major holidays," she explains. "I didn't grow up with too much of a religious background, so I really never read about miracles and other supernatural happenings that the Bible talks about. The miracles came later in my life."

The elder of two children, for most of Alpha's growing-up years she often had to play the role of mother and father to her younger brother because her parents were always busy struggling to provide for their family. Alpha decided early in life to earn lots of money when she grew older to make up for all the deprivation she and her family had suffered over the years. With her family now living in New York City, Alpha began her career path by majoring in accounting at St. John's University.

When she graduated in 1994 she went into private accounting work at Morgan Stanley Dean Witter, a firm that occupied about 60 percent of the office space at Tower Two of the World Trade Center. Alpha was twenty-two years old when she started, and she thought that working at the Twin Towers was a most exciting opportunity — even though the first terrorist attack on the World Trade Center, a bombing by Islamic militants, was still recent. Alpha is grateful she wasn't working in the building at that time, because she would likely have been in an office that was severely damaged, given the space that the firm she later joined occupied.

Alpha's salary was lucrative. She was doing investment management and she was a young rising star. She worked in that environment for seven years, racking up promotions and earning more and more money. "I was driven by the corporate world and that's all I knew. There was absolutely nothing spiritual going on in my life," she describes.

But in 2000 a new dimension in her life would begin to unfold through an accidental encounter with a woman who would become her spiritual mentor. This woman was her aunt's teacher and her mother's guest.

"Right from the beginning she influenced my life quite radically," Alpha says. Alpha became interested in the power of thought, and her mentor gave her several books to read by a Bulgarian spiritual master. "I started reading three or four of these books and I just ate it up," she declares. "Then I started looking for more of his books and none of the big chains carried it. I now really wanted to know more about spiritual life."

Alpha began to pray that she would meet a spiritual teacher like the master whose books she had read. "I felt I needed contact — I needed a dialogue. I loved what I was reading and my life started to change. I didn't know at the time that I had already met the spiritual master I was praying for—the woman in my mother's kitchen."

Alpha had another opportunity to meet with this remarkable woman whose name she declines to disclose. "She's a very humble and modest woman and she's not seeking any kind of publicity," she explains. "In talking to her, faith started to develop in me. I started understanding that there's more than just the physical body and there was more to life than just trying to make money. Now that I was being introduced to my spiritual side, I began to realize that my whole life was selfish and materialistic."

As what Alpha considers the miraculous transformation in her life continued, so did her conversations with her new spiritual master. Now, going to work at the World Trade Center no longer was as exciting or meaningful to her as it once had been.

Alpha recollects that a year before the September 11 disaster she came to a momentous decision that she firmly believes was God-sent. "I consulted with my teacher and made a decision that wasn't very easy to make—but it was one that I consider a miracle because it saved my life," she attests. "This was just at a time when my boss was telling me, 'You have such great potential that you'll be making treasure soon.' He then promoted me to vice president of one of the divisions."

Despite the salary increase and prestige of her new position, Alpha resigned from the firm. It was a decision she is convinced saved her life. "As I began to understand more and more about what the true meaning of life is and what my true goal is in this life, I couldn't see myself managing assets and being in the position I was," she submits. "So I quit and then I traveled for a while to do some soul-searching and see what it was that I wanted to do."

Alpha gives a lot of credit to her spiritual master. "Over the years I've witnessed her perform hundreds of miracles—including healings," she asserts. "She doesn't perform miracles by touch, but by helping people understand that there is God in each one of us and by expanding their God consciousness.

"One of the miracles she performed was the miracle of my own transformation," she continues. "She helped me to understand the real reason why a person was created. Now, I was feeling more spiritual than ever before. I had the faith that God would guide me. I was sure He would lead me into doing something that would give back to Him."

When the World Trade Center was attacked, Alpha watched the tragedy unfold on television in complete shock. The very office that she had worked in was struck by the hijacked airliner. Only then, she says, did she understand the enormity of the miracle that had been granted her.

"I had moved from a life that was not filled with spirit to finding a teacher who opened me up spiritually and guided me away from the material world I was then involved with," she professes. "Then, through prayer, I had moved into a more spiritual relationship with God. I believe that as a result of this new life He gave me the miracle of saving my life."

Today, an extremely grateful Alpha believes that her primary mission is to share the knowledge of wise spiritual teachers from many different religious traditions, which is why she opened a bookstore that offers metaphysical titles in Manhattan's East Village area. "The store certainly isn't materially rewarding yet, but that's not its focus," she says.

"There are so many other rewards I get from what I've created here. Every time someone walks in I know I'm helping to influence their life. So many people have told me how their lives have changed from reading one of the books we sell here. And that fulfills me immensely."

*I*t was one of those typical midwestern winter days, and Jennifer Kohrman, then a Fort Wayne, Indiana, college student, recalls feeling about as miserable as the weather. It was January 2, 1999, and the twenty-three-year-old was brooding about what to do with her life when she graduated in May.

A psychology major, she was considering applying for graduate school and entering a school counseling program. But she didn't feel sure it was what God wanted her to do with her life.

Jennifer had always been religious. Her parents

were devout Catholics and the family went to church regularly, where Jennifer found miracle stories completely absorbing. She was always active and involved in church activities.

Jennifer prayed for direction. God seemed to remain silent. Christmas and New Year's came, but the joy of the holidays couldn't dispel her confusion. She wondered if God was really concerned about her at all.

In order to help pay her college tuition, Jennifer was working at the time in the produce department of a local grocery store, alongside her younger sister, Kathy. On January 2, a Saturday, Jennifer and Kathy were both scheduled to work. The weather forecasters had warned the residents of northeastern Indiana of a severe snowstorm moving into the area.

When Jennifer and Kathy arrived at work, there was already a light snowfall. The storm worsened as the morning progressed, and driving conditions were hazardous. At about 10:30, the two young women received permission from their manager to leave early and go home. They decided to take a road back where there wouldn't be a lot of hills and turns, a straight path to their home.

An east-west highway, Dupont Road was normally heavily traveled, but during the snowstorm it was completely empty. Kathy's white Cavalier was about half a mile from the store when they experienced a whiteout.

Kathy veered off the road, narrowly missing a telephone pole, then landed in a ditch. Both sisters were shaken up, terrified at what had almost happened.

Jennifer regained her composure first, and she got out of the car to look around. Although it had only been snowing for a few hours, there was already a five-inch cover of snow on the ground. The car was stuck. There was no way Jennifer and Kathy could push it back onto the road.

"Kathy, we're pretty much stuck here," said Jennifer as she got back into the car.

"Jen, I'm really scared. What are we going to do?" said the younger sister.

They were abandoned on an empty highway without a cell phone. Jennifer looked searchingly in both directions, and there wasn't anyone in sight. She thought of starting out on foot, but she didn't want to leave Kathy all alone. So she did the only thing she could think of: She bowed her head and silently began to pray: "Please, God, help us."

A few seconds passed. Jennifer looked up, and to her amazement, there was a white four-by-four utility vehicle parked right next to them.

Jennifer says her first reaction was, "Wow, this is cool. He answered my prayers. Thank God." A man climbed out of the vehicle and came over. He stood next to the passenger side door and asked, "Are both of you all right?"

Jennifer responded in the affirmative, saying they were both a little shaken up because they had almost hit a telephone pole when they landed in the ditch.

The man said, "Okay, just wait here," and then he got on his CB radio and summoned a man who was plowing a housing addition down the road, and he came to help them out. They attached a rope to the back of the Cavalier and pulled them out of the ditch.

The man told them to drive to a nearby neighborhood until they had calmed down and felt they could make the drive home. "It was good advice," Jennifer says, because they were both still frightened and jittery. Jennifer and Kathy thanked the two men for their kindness and went home about five minutes later, grateful and relieved.

Today, Jennifer, who recently graduated from Indiana University with her master's degree in School Consulting, believes she and her sister were the recipients of a miracle that stormy day. "Even though I have no proof that the man who helped us was an actual angel, what is miraculous is how quickly God responded to my prayers and sent someone to help us when we desperately needed it," she declares.

"I consider the experience a miracle. It made me realize how much God really does care about each one of us. It makes me feel confident that He does watch out for people in trouble, the way He did for me and my sister." Jennifer has never doubted again.

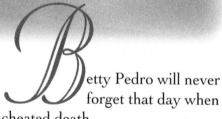

etty Pedro will never forget that day when her husband, Don, cheated death.

On a warm Saturday afternoon in May, Don, who was a firefighter, went into the firehouse to cover for someone who was ill. Betty and the kids were at home and going about their normal life, as Betty describes it. The kids were cleaning their rooms, and Betty was doing housework.

While driving to the Endicott Fire Department Local 1280, Don found something wrong with his car. So during his lunch hour he decided to look underneath it. He took a tire off.

Suddenly the jack bent at a ninety-degree angle and Don was trapped under the car for approximately twenty minutes until one of the firemen came down from upstairs and found Don pinned under the car.

Don is white, but his skin looked black. The firefighter and others who arrived on the scene could detect no pulse and no heartbeat, but they were able to resuscitate Don at the firehouse and get him on a breathing device. Then he was rushed to the hospital.

Betty heard the report over the fire department scanner her husband kept in the house. She dropped everything, leaving the kids at her mother's house, and rushed over to the hospital. She can't even remember the drive. "I just wanted to get there. But I knew by the tone of the fireman's voice on the scanner that things were not good."

Betty stayed in the waiting room for a long time, and then the priest showed up from their parish. Betty knew it wasn't a good sign. When the doctor finally came in, he told Betty it didn't look good at all. He didn't expect Don to make it through the night. Don had been deprived of oxygen for so long and the coma was so deep that his chances of survival were very thin.

That's when the New York State housewife began praying.

The first miracle was that Don survived the night. The next day Betty received a call from Don's captain's mother, who said that while in a prayer group she had a vision in which Jesus kissed Don's head. The woman, whose name was also Betty, didn't know what it meant.

After she heard about the vision, Betty got down on her knees, and prayed. She asked God for a sign.

Returning the next morning to her husband's room in the intensive care unit, Betty took his hand. To her surprise, he squeezed back. Betty knew it was the sign she had just been praying for, even though the doctor told her it was only an involuntary response. Betty laughs now, remembering. "Every time he moved they said it was an involuntary response. But I knew differently."

When doctors tested the then-thirty-nine-year-old firefighter's brain waves, the results were sluggish. They told Betty this was not a good sign. He might open his eyes; he might raise his arm—but that's all he would ever do again. They asked if Betty wanted to take him off the respirator, but she refused. "I just knew deep inside that he was there. I used to sit in his room and sing 'Amazing Grace' to him." Betty was not surprised to see that her husband's heartbeat would increase whenever she sang that hymn.

Betty pointed out the increase to her husband's doctors, but they remained skeptical. "Everything to them was 'involuntary response,'" she declares. "The doctors knew that when a man goes without oxygen for twenty minutes, he dies. Nothing else could sway their opinions."

For two weeks, Don held on, while Betty prayed. Since Betty wouldn't take him off the respirator, the doctors decided to try radical surgery. Betty gave permission, and, in preparation for the surgery, Don received a feeding tube and a tracheotomy. But the very day the surgery was scheduled, Don started breathing on his own.

Don's doctors admitted that they were shocked. Betty wasn't shocked at all. "From where I saw it, there were signs of his recovery every step of the way," she declares. "The doctors just didn't see it."

Don was transferred to the brain injury unit at Binghamton General Hospital. Two days later, he spoke. Soon he was speaking sentences. One of the doctors from Williams Memorial Hospital, where Don had been originally, came to Betty and gave her a big hug. He said, "You know, you really opened my eyes. I would never have believed that your husband would survive, but you never gave up hope." Betty told him that he had witnessed a miracle, and that God had walked with her and Don every step of the way.

Even Betty was shocked one morning, when Don had completely recovered his ability to speak. "You know Betty, dear, I knew it wasn't time for me to die because I had a dream that Jesus came and kissed me on the head," Don told her.

Betty was shocked to realize that Don had experienced the same vision that his captain's mother had seen just two days after the accident. "Two people had this same vision. I really do believe that Jesus came to him," says Betty.

The retired firefighter continues to make excellent progress with his recovery. He can walk—with assistance—and speak and play with his children.

Don's miracle survival was reported in newspapers, magazines, and on television news shows throughout the nation. "Thousands of people heard his story," she says. "His survival has been an inspiration to many people. What happened to us had brought a lot of people back to their faith, because he really came back from the dead. It was a miracle."

For anyone who has a loved one in critical condition, Betty urges them never to give up hope. "Keep praying," she says. "I believe that if you do, God will give you a sign and show you what you need."

*J*erry Pae considers himself the least likely person to be granted the gift of healing by God. As a child, he went to Catholic school, but he felt alienated from the Church. "They started the Mass by asking for money and finished up with more requests for cash. It always seemed to me like the service was a trap to get you in the door so they could ask and ask and ask for money," Jerry says.

Jerry isn't a churchgoer to this day. But he concedes that something profound has taken hold of his soul and has changed his life. "I now think of life and other things in a whole new light," he asserts. "How couldn't I after what happened to me?"

On a cool fall day in 1999, Jerry recalls that he was driving to work, his mind filled with unhappy thoughts. His father had recently died from cancer, and, his mother, Nora, had been diagnosed with bone cancer. She was slowly succumbing to this very painful disease.

"When my father died, on his deathbed he asked me to take care of Mom," he relates. "And I was kind of thinking about that as I was driving to my office. As I was driving, I saw a baby deer by the side of the road. It was very bloody and obviously had been whacked by a car. I could even smell that dead animal smell coming off him."

Jerry drove past the dead deer without stopping. Returning home from work about ten hours later, he noticed the deer again. "The deer was still lying there with its eyes closed," he relates. "Nothing had changed.

"This is where it gets weird," Jerry admits. As he drove past the deer, what he describes as "a warm feeling" came over him all of a sudden. "It was like somebody had turned the heater on in my car. All of a sudden I was getting these memories of my father. I just felt very 'spiritual'—I can't think of any other word for it. I don't know why, but I just decided, 'Let me take care of this little feller,' and so I turned my car around and went back to the deer."

Jerry pulled his car over to the side of the road and approached the apparently dead animal. "He certainly looked like a goner to me. He had been there all day and there was no movement. His eyes were shut, blood was dried on the road that had come from its mouth, and he was cold to the touch."

Jerry dragged the animal off the side of the road and examined it for a minute. Then he grabbed the deer's head and held it for a few seconds. Again, he was overcome by an unusual warm sensation. Then something miraculous happened.

All of a sudden, the deer came to life. "It startled the hell out of me," Jerry recalls. The animal stood up, and shook itself. Then it gave Jerry a look that he is convinced spoke of gratitude. Then it bolted off into the woods. "As God is my witness, this happened," says Jerry. "And I know that deer was d-e-a-d."

Jerry is unable to explain exactly what happened that day. "I got this feeling about my father; then this warm feeling swept over me, and the next thing I know I'm holding this deer's head for a few moments and it comes back to life!"

Jerry couldn't even bring himself to tell his wife about it. That next morning he decided to stop by his mother's house. As he embraced his mother, she hugged him back very tightly. He felt the same warm spiritual feeling come over him, and he was acting in ways he couldn't explain once again. He held his mother by the head—as he had done to the deer—and told her he loved her. She said, "Jerry, whenever I hold your hand I think of Dad."

Then Jerry had a scare. His mother fainted in the hallway and was out of it for ten minutes or so. He had to call 911. An ambulance took her to the hospital, even though they could find nothing wrong with her.

A few days later came the revelation. Jerry's mother went to her doctor's office at the Cleveland Clinic for her regular checkup, and her bone cancer was gone without a trace. She had been dying of the disease, and now she was perfectly healthy.

When Jerry told the doctors at the hospital about the incident involving the deer and then his mother, he says they said nothing. "They certainly believed in positive attitude helping a person get well—but answered prayers and miracles was a bit too far out for them."

To this day, Jerry says that whenever he thinks about those two unusual days in his life, all he can do is shake his head in wonder. "I don't know if or why I was a vessel for these miracles," he submits. "Maybe skeptics can explain the deer away by saying it was never dead. But could my mom be misdiagnosed by one of the world's leading cancer hospitals—the Cleveland Clinic? She had also been to every other doctor in town who knew about her condition—the same doctors as my dad had."

One explanation that Jerry offers is that his father's spirit had entered him. "I associate that thought with the end result," he says. "I also think that the Lord gives you the power to do things—that all the tools to heal really are within you—and although we have the knowledge and ability to heal ourselves and others we don't use those powers. Maybe it happened to me because I was told by my father to take care of Mom, and somehow that deer activated that power. Or it just simply was a miracle. I just don't know."

Jerry's mother had several more good years. She is now ailing again, with a different medical condition. Although he hugs her each day, so far there has been no repeat of the life-saving miracle that he once performed.

Reflecting back on those days in 1999, Jerry asserts: "I don't feel any more religious than I used to. I still have skepticism about the Catholic Church. But I sure feel more than ever that's there something up there. I'm taking better care of people in my life since then, and I'm loving people better as a result of that experience."

im Carter had always wanted to be a minister, and he held a ministerial degree from the Quaker-sponsored John Wesley Bible College. But he married and had two children, and he and his wife never figured out a way to make ends meet on a minister's salary. So he had a position in marketing and sales and his adored wife owned a store. It was, he says, "a very full, rich, and beautiful life."

This richness started from Tim's love for his wife, Terry. She was the love of his life. They had been high school sweethearts. "I fell in love with her from the first time I saw her at my high school Bible club. 'Tim and Terry' seemed to naturally go together and I had no other vision for my life other than Terry and I pursuing our future enthusiastically and growing old, together."

So nothing could terrify Tim more than the events of September 1998. Terry was supposed to meet him for dinner at a restaurant, but there was a sign on the door that the restaurant was closed for repairs.

Tim went in search of Terry, his fear growing. But he couldn't find her. When Tim went home there were many messages on the machine. "At first they didn't make any sense to me," says Tim. It sounded like Terry had been in an accident. No sooner did he hear the messages than the phone rang again.

It was one of Tim's best friends. Terry had been in a terrible accident and he'd better hurry over to the hospital, the friend told him. Before he could even get off the phone, it rang again—it was the police asking him to wait at home. They said they'd come over and escort Tim to the hospital. He said, "You're going to have to race me there." Tim left his elder son in charge, "and who knows what thoughts were going on in my head as I raced over there," Tim says.

A big man weighing more than 280 pounds, the minister recalls that "when I came through the doors of that hospital I probably looked like a bull in a China shop.

They told me I had to wait before I went back to see my wife—but I didn't wait at all."

Terry was lying unconscious in her hospital room. She had been driving Tim's Mazda truck instead of her own Explorer. There was a deer stand in the back of the truck that Tim used for hunting, and someone in town she knew had asked her to demonstrate how it worked. She got up there without knowing what she was doing, and she fell sixteen feet out of the truck.

The neurosurgeon told Tim that in a technical sense Terry had already died. She sustained a fatal brain injury and nothing could be done for her. "I was crying. I was in convulsions. I felt like I was dying," says Tim. He had lost his father only a few months earlier. The possibility of losing the woman he'd loved since he was seventeen was unbearable.

Tim admits to grabbing the surgeon and begging him to do something. "You have in your care the most beautiful, precious person you have ever medically treated. You have to do something."

Moved, the surgeon promised he would conduct one additional test that was outside the normal routine. If Terry responded, he would operate. He didn't expect any response. Tim recalls sitting in the waiting room praying "with every fiber of my being." The neurosurgeon brought the news that Terry had, indeed, responded positively to the test. An operation would be scheduled.

Tim's relief was short-lived. Terry came through the surgery so poorly the neurosurgeon expected her to die "within seconds, minutes, or a few hours." The official medical report was already written and signed by the surgeon. It said, "Precursor brain death."

Tim's pastor was with him when Tim learned of the medical report. Tim was blind with grief. "I was out of my mind," he somberly recalls. Pastor McDaniels held Tim, restraining him. He said, "Tim, God's not asking you to understand right now, just to trust."

Those words were just what he needed, Tim recalls. "It kept me from turning away from God because I was so angry at what had happened to Terry. The minute he said that, it was like being on a diving board, and I just jumped into the arms of Jesus."

The nurses wanted to know if Tim wanted to donate her organs. "As long as there is one hope in heaven or earth, we will not talk about donating her organs. It's my understanding that she's still functioning on some level," Tim told the nurse.

Tim knew that, as much as the hospital staff was moved by his feelings, no one at the hospital believed there was any hope that Terry would survive.

But a deluge of sympathy joined Tim's hope. Various

newspapers reported on Terry's dramatic struggle, publishing steady updates on her condition. Thousands of people throughout the country were praying for her.

The doctors at the hospital were steadfast in their belief that nothing could help Terry. For two weeks Tim heard that his wife would not survive. As she clung to life for those weeks, they began to say—unanimously—that even if she did survive, she would never be anything more than a "vegetable."

As the days and weeks passed, Tim spent enormous amounts of time down on his knees asking God for help. The elders of his church joined him sometimes. "I prayed, 'God, just let her be happy again. Don't let her just exist in some vegetative state.' I was there around the clock praying for her. I put Christian music and Scripture tapes in her room, twenty-four hours a day," says Tim.

The prognosis for Terry's recovery remained grim. The swelling in her brain went down, but the doctors still did not believe that Terry could improve enough to be even eligible for a rehabilitation center. There was no hope of her survival or recovery. But Tim still believed in God and miracles, and he told everyone so.

One day when Tim visited his wife after her surgery, he felt especially distraught. "There was no life in her," he recalls. Her head was shaved for the surgery. "You can't imagine looking at someone that you've loved your whole life and she being just like a rock. I just stood there and cried and continued to pray with all my might and all my heart."

The days continued to pass and Terry showed no signs of improvement. Her eyes were always closed, the coma unrelenting.

There was one day when several reporters interviewed him. As Tim describes it, "One of them asked me if I was being realistic in my hope for a recovery. I told him, 'I'm not out of touch with reality like the doctors are telling me.' I said, 'In my mind God has already performed a miracle.'"

Tim was not speaking idly. Each time he visited his wife's room, he could feel "a genuine presence of God," he says. "Everybody in the hospital could tell you that there was a spiritual healing atmosphere in that room. Even the nurses on duty could tell you that. That room was charged with God's power. Everybody noticed it and everybody commented on it."

Finally, there came the day when Tim firmly believes all the prayers and faith in his wife's spiritual recovery were finally manifested. "I walked into the room and Terry suddenly opened her eyes. I felt like a schoolboy. I went running to the church and shouting with joy and telling everyone that Terry had opened her eyes. I was so excited. The whole church was in pandemonium. Everyone believed they had witnessed a miracle beyond a shadow of any doubt."

Terry's eventual recovery was not an instant miracle story. "It was a roller coaster ride," he says. "Some days she would be holding my hand, and some days she couldn't hold my hand anymore and went back to just a blank stare. Meanwhile, the doctors were still predicting that in the best of all worlds she would be in a vegetative state and never again be able to understand anything."

Again, he recalls, doctors were urging him to pull the plug on his wife's life support system. And, again, he refused to do so. "One day a doctor with a Middle Eastern accent came into her room, looked at me, and said, 'There's no decision for you to make. God's already made it.'" To Tim's amazement, the doctor took Terry off the ventilator, put her on another breathing machine, and told her husband, "She'll survive." Her neurosurgeon had suggested that Tim let her go just the day before.

The next day, Terry took a spoon to feed herself. That very same day, her mother came into the room to pray for her, and Terry closed her eyes to pray along. "It was small miracle after small miracle leading to bigger ones," says Tim. "It took months for her to recover, but the degree of her recovery was truly miraculous."

On the day that Terry was checked out of the hospital, one of the most skeptical of the neurosurgeons approached him. The doctor said, "You know, what happened here was a miracle."

Today, Tim describes Terry as a "bright, sweet person who inspires many." She walks without a cane, although she is severely impaired on her right side. "And she has recovered her incredibly pleasant personality," says her loving husband, "Though she can say only a few words that can be understood."

Terry has to take anti-seizure medication for the rest of her life. Her difficulties with communication are frustrating. Yet she sings in church, and can tell the people she loves how she feels. She is, Tim says, "a million miles from vegetative or bedridden as the doctors said she would be."

Tim describes all that happened as bittersweet. "Even though her degree of recovery is truly miraculous, Terry is not the same wife and mother she was before. Before the accident she taught children to read, did Christian clown performances, and starred in our church play, which nine-thousand people came to see annually. She did tons of arts and crafts and was truly one of the most creative and outgoing people you can imagine.

"So a miracle has taken place, but there has also been much heartache, loss, and pain. Not only was Terry's life devastated by the accident, but it ruined me financially and made it necessary for me to raise the children by myself."

But Tim's dream has come true because of the accident: He is now a full-time Quaker minister. "In spite of the pain and sacrifice, we have all witnessed God's providential care. Yes, things have been tough since the accident," he concludes, "but we are living proof that even the most devastating event can turn out for good when people turn to God. One of those 'good' things is I then decided once and for all to devote myself full-time to my ministry."

Rev. Carter is eager to share his testimony so that others can learn from it. "Because of the pain associated with talking about the events that happened back then I never did," he asserts. "However, I now feel it is the right time and that others might be blessed and inspired by hearing our story."

When Judy Houck discovered a lump in her breast one evening in 1984, she was terrified. She remembers murmuring a plea for help immediately: "Devil get behind me in Jesus' name." She showed her husband, John, what she had found, but he didn't say a word. The two, who had been married for twenty-five years and shared five children, just stared at each other. "We both knew what this was, but we did not put a name to it," Judy explains.

Judy believes that people are often too quick to name their diseases. "When you name it, it gets worse," she declares. For a week Judy refused to go see a doctor. But her children found out and they began to plead with her to go get help.

Judy went for an examination, and testing showed that the lump was malignant. But she was reluctant to get treatment. After all, it was God she had come to rely on over the years—not doctors. "I'd been serving God for over forty years," she exclaims, "and have been in the ministry for over thirty-six wonderful years. My husband and I had relied solely upon faith in God."

The singer and minister, who, with her husband, today operates the Wings of Healing Ministries and the Gospel Tabernacle Assembly Church—both in Gastonia, North Carolina—candidly admits that her faith was not always so solid.

Although she grew up the daughter of a Presbyterian minister, Judy recollects that there was not much religious talk around the dinner table. Her mother was not overly religious, and this set the tone.

But Judy met John and they settled down to raise a family in Gastonia. One night, John, who at the time was earning a living working odd jobs, had a religious vision—one that led him to become a preacher. It was this renewal of her husband's faith that eventually revived Judy's. Since that day, Judy and John have walked closely with the Lord. In fact, Judy had spent the evening performing gospel music on the night she first found the lump.

Judy admits that despite her strong faith she was frightened. The minute she and John walked out of her doctor's office when the diagnosis was confirmed, Judy turned her face to heaven and declared a fifteen-day fast to God. She went home to pray. "Despite my fear, I knew that was the real solution to my problem."

Judy believes she experienced a miracle five days into her fast. "I had this sensation that is still difficult for me to explain," she relates. "I just knew that something was happening inside my body. I knew with certainty that God was doing something for me. I even told my daughter and my husband how I felt. They were all for it—my whole family was and my church was very supportive. And it was at that very moment when I experienced this feeling that I claimed my healing."

A few days later Judy found herself in the office of a cancer specialist at the nearby Gaston Memorial Hospital. She recalls that when she told the specialist about her healing, he responded without enthusiasm. He told her very bluntly that she had about three months to live and that surgery was her only chance.

The doctor told her about chemotherapy. He warned

her that it would cause bleeding from her kidneys and colon and then vomiting. He also said that once she began the chemotherapy she would lose all of her hair. "He gave me all the bad news he could tell me," says Judy.

Instead of frightening her, Judy recollects that the specialist's words made her fighting mad. "I had just experienced the greatest peace of God and was waiting for my miracle, and I wasn't going to listen to that kind of talk. I looked at my doctor and I said, 'I'm not going to die. I'm going to live.'"

Judy underwent surgery shortly after Christmas. When the surgeon looked inside her, he was shocked. Surrounding the tumor was what he could only describe as a "shield"—a fleshy covering that blocked the cancer from spreading directly into the bloodstream. The surgeon admitted he never had seen anything like that in all the years of doing cancer surgery. It became the talk of the hospital. He said that the only explanation he had was that some "higher power" had placed that shield there to protect her.

When the tumor was removed, Judy reluctantly began chemotherapy treatment. She believed that God had already healed her, but she began radiation and started taking seven pills a day.

The therapy nearly killed her. By the end of the week Judy was at death's door. She was bleeding and had blisters inside her mouth. "I felt like my body was on fire," says Judy.

That following Monday Judy returned to her cancer specialist and couldn't believe what he told her. He said that he had overdosed her. He had given her enough chemicals to kill her. The doctor gave Judy a blood test.

The results were entirely contrary to his expectation. Judy was showing rapid improvement. "Praise the Lord," Judy said to the nurse. "He's healed me and I don't need these chemotherapy treatments any longer."

The nurse began to cry with joy. She said, "I'm so glad." Judy went to the front desk, paid her bill, and told the receptionist that she wouldn't be back.

The doctor rushed out. He said that if the surgeon had missed removing any cancer cells, she would die without chemotherapy treatments. Judy was unmoved. As she walked out of the door she had an overwhelming feeling of peace—a sensation that her body was completely healed.

When Judy returned home and told her family about her decision not to continue treatment, they rejoiced with her. The shield around the cancer had convinced them that God was working miracles. "We all know, Mama, that you're not gonna die—that you're gonna live," said one of Judy's daughters.

Judy had lost nearly all of her hair, and she was still

feeling weak from the too-strong chemotherapy treatments. Both those conditions quickly improved. In a few days she was feeling much stronger and her hair was growing back. "My body was waking up. It was God healing me. I went back to teaching Sunday school, singing, and praising the Lord." Eighteen years later, Judy says her hair is thick and strong, and she's healthier than ever.

*C*harlie Whitehorse wrestled with it for a long time. He had planned to be an electrical engineer—a career for which he had earned a degree and that would provide a stable income so he could help his mother. But he had felt a strong pull when some elders at the Seventh-day Adventist Church, where he had attended since his conversion to Christianity in high school, said they needed the help of youthful pastors to minister to the Navajo tribe. He had always been aware that there was a void in his life that electrical engineering simply couldn't fill.

Charlie decided he would follow the path God had set out for him, going to a Seventh-day Adventist Bible College in California to study to become a pastor, but he asked the Creator to look after his mother while he was away from their home on a Navajo Indian reservation in Monument Valley, Utah, studying. "Lord, I want you to look after my mom while I'm at school in California. I don't want you to let anything happen to her," he prayed.

Charlie's first quarter at school passed without incident. "I came home from school and shared everything that I was doing. We were all very excited, and everyone was proud and happy for me—especially my mother." Charlie's mother, Susie, had been his inspiration in becoming a Christian. She converted when he was seven and his initial conversion—the family's spiritual practice had been based around Indian religion prior to this time—was done more to please his mother than to fulfill an inner need. But in high school, Charlie became a committed Christian. Now faith was something Charlie could share with his mother, and she was bursting with pride.

Two months later, in February, Charlie's sister called him at school. Their mother was in the hospital and had suffered a stroke.

Feeling that God had disappointed him, Charlie called the hospital and got nothing but bad news. A nurse told him that his mother was in critical condition and might not make it. "This really shook me. I had never experienced anything like this before," he says.

The nurse also told Charlie that his mother required immediate surgery. She would need either a heart transplant or a pacemaker. "I just listened, said nothing, and felt there was a real possibility that I was going to lose my mother," Charlie remembers.

Despite his feeling of being disappointed by the Lord's failure to protect Susie absolutely, Charlie didn't give up on God. "I immediately began praying for her. My friends at school and people on the reservation also started praying for her," he says.

A week later, Susie was still clinging to life. Although the doctors were still urging him to allow them to perform surgery, the pastor says he delayed doing so because he believed more in prayer than in medicine. He did approve his mother's transfer to another hospital in Tucson, Arizona, which specialized in heart surgeries. It was shortly afterward that he firmly believes a miracle took place.

"During this time hundreds of people were praying for my mother and I was receiving lots of encouragement from my friends at school. Nobody knew what the outcome would be, but we all kept our faith in God's healing powers," says Charlie.

As a routine matter, the hospital in Tucson gave Susie a battery of cardiac tests, never expecting to find anything but confirmation of what the other hospital had found.

But Susie's heart was functioning in a perfectly normal manner. Every test showed the same thing. The doctors told her that her heart was strong.

There was nothing wrong with her. Susie could go home—she didn't need any surgery. "They said they couldn't even understand why she was even sent to them," says Rev. Whitehorse. They flew her back to the original hospital, where the testing was repeated. Her heart was perfectly normal.

News of Susie's miraculous recovery awed the Indian tribe, Rev. Whitehorse recalls. Christians and non-Christians alike joined in praise of God. One of Susie's brothers, who hadn't been a Christian, started going to church for the first time.

Upon receiving news of his mother's miraculous recovery, Rev. Whitehorse attests that he fell down on his knees to thank God. "It was an incredible relief to me and a validation of my faith," he professes. "It was a real test of faith for me. I think God was trying to find out how serious I was about serving Him and pursuing a ministry.

"It could've been easy for me to quit the ministry

because I believed God had promised that He would protect my mother while I was away at school, but she got sick, anyway. Instead, I hung in there. The whole experience strengthened my faith and my walk with the Lord. Not only did He show me there was a real God, but he also demonstrated that miracles do happen."

*P*amela Strong came home from school one day in 1987 complaining of a stomachache.

The high school senior and member of the National Honor Society was also running a low-grade fever, and her mother, Susan, told her that if the fever continued the next day, she would not be going to school.

"Pam gave me a big argument," Susan says. "She was having midterms and felt that she couldn't miss school." But the next morning Pamela was too weak to get out of bed. She was vomiting. Her mother and grandmother, who lived with them, had to dress Pam like a two-year-old because she couldn't do anything for herself.

Pam's condition continued to grow worse. Her temperature had spiked. Her mother took her to the doctor, and she vomited all the way to the doctor's office. He took one look at the weakened teenager and said, "Take her to the emergency room."

Susan and her mother rushed Pam over to Burlington Memorial Hospital in New Jersey, where a spinal tap was conducted. The results of the test were terrifying. Doctors diagnosed the teenager with a severe case of spinal meningitis.

"I just couldn't believe it," Susan declares. Pamela had been the picture of health a couple of days earlier. The seventeen-year-old was admitted to the hospital, and by that evening the prognosis did not look good.

A day or so later, the news got even worse. It was a Saturday when Susan received a phone call telling her that her daughter was dying. The hospital told her to prepare for the end. The disease had progressed into Pam's brain stem and encephalitis was developing. Her brain was starting to swell.

All Susan can recall of that moment is thinking that God must have a plan for her daughter to allow this to happen. "I have a strong belief in the afterlife," she declares, "and I felt that if my daughter was going to be taken at such a young age, it's like a gardener moving a tender plant to another location where it will bloom even better. And yet as a mother I didn't want to lose my baby—so I had very conflicting emotions at that moment."

At the time of Pam's ordeal, Susan and Pam were practicing the Baha'i faith. "Pam was not raised rigidly as a Baha'i," Susan explains. "She was also exposed to Christianity, Muslim, and Buddhist beliefs. She was a much more spiritual person than my husband and I were and was always studying the works of different religions. But she was especially active in the Baha'i faith, attending youth conferences and everything."

Upon receiving that dreadful telephone call, Susan immediately contacted her daughter's school and friends to fill them in on the situation. As Baha'is, she and Pam had connections to all different religions, so she was pleased to have her daughters friends saying prayers for Pam in synagogues, Catholic and Protestant churches, Mosques, and Hindu temples. There were prayers being said for her at Mount Carmel in Haifa at the Baha'i World Center.

Susan says that by Sunday she, her ex-husband, and the rest of the family were all pretty much resigned to Pam's death. "We all knew we were going to lose her and didn't think she was going to make it through the weekend."

But Pam got through Sunday night. By Monday morning, something special started to take shape. Susan went to the hospital and Pam was sitting up in bed. She said she didn't even remember being taken to the hospital. She also said she was hungry.

The doctors were amazed. There were no signs, no symptoms—not a trace of the disease. It had simply vanished. "There's no doubt in my mind that all the prayer for her had created this miracle," says Susan.

Susan says that her daughter—now a healthy thirty-three-year-old homemaker living in San Francisco with her two children—"was such a spiritual child to begin with that her goodness came through to other people. People responded to her and their prayers weren't just lip service. These were deeply felt prayers from the heart."

The memory of the day of Pam's discharge from the hospital brings a chuckle to Susan's lips. "On the discharge slip all they put was 'stomach virus.' They didn't know what else to put. The doctors were all amazed that my daughter had made a complete recovery."

Susan believes that her daughter's recovery was a message from God. "Pam doesn't remember much of what happened to her," she says, "but we've discussed many times why God had given her a reprieve. I firmly believe my daughter has a mission in life—that there's something God wants her to do."

As for herself, she says that Pam's miraculous healing convinces her more than ever that God works wonders and responds to prayer. "All I can say for sure is 'yes, I believe in miracles.' because I've experienced one . . ."

$\mathcal{G}$raham Pockett was due to pick up his wife, Margaret, from their pastor's house where she had been attending a women's meeting at around noon on that cool and sunny winter's day. Running a few minutes late, Graham, who lives about an hour north of Sydney, Australia, tripped on a loose board along a timber path. At about 260 pounds, Graham fell heavily, and awkwardly. His hand was partially outstretched but his little finger still curled into the palm of his hand. He took the entire weight on the side of his left hand. He knew he had broken his wrist.

Graham is no stranger to broken bones. "I've broken many of them over the years," he submits. "The last time I broke an arm was in nineteen sixty-eight when I had a motorcycle accident." Graham was lying on the ground and he couldn't move. He was experiencing symptoms of shock.

Graham's wife and all the women from the meeting rushed out to help him, and one woman started praying. Soon they were all praying.

Graham started praying, too, hoping that his wrist or hand was not broken because he knew how it would affect his work — Graham worked full-time on the Internet creating a freeware-only Web site.

Graham was hoisted onto a chair. "I looked at my wrist and it had this unnatural *Z* shape," he recollects. "My little finger was protruding from my hand at nearly ninety degrees. Boy, I thought, this doesn't look good. Wrists are not supposed to have extra bends in them."

With his left arm cradled in a makeshift sling, Graham went with Margaret to Gosford Hospital, the largest local hospital in the area. The nurse who examined him said he had a radial shaft fracture. She explained that he had snapped both the bones in his forearm. Graham and his wife waited an hour for the doctor to appear. They spent some of that time silently praying together.

Graham examined his wrist again at one point and was surprised by what he saw. The unnatural bend in his wrist had gone. It was straight and normal.

"I was absolutely amazed," Graham says. "This was impossible. Broken wrists do not repair themselves within an hour—not without something miraculous happening. I guess I hoped that God would mend the broken wrist, but I never really expected that He would.

"I had seen some other miraculous things over the years, but nothing like this had ever happened to me. Up until that time I could accept by faith that miracles happen, but it hadn't penetrated my logical mind that it would ever happen to me."

When the doctor, who had yet to see Graham's hand, called him into the examining room, Graham said all he saw was his little finger protruding at an unusual angle. "He declared there were broken bones in my hand and ordered an x-ray."

By now, two and a half hours had passed. When the doctor examined the report from the radiologist, Graham recalls that the physician looked startled. "The report from the radiologist was amazing because there was no sign of any break in the hand or wrist! Apart from some swelling, by the next day I was able to continue working on my Web site."

To this day, Graham's amazement is as strong as it

ever was. "I have no doubts that God healed my wrist and hand that day," he proclaims. "The wrist had a definite—and unnatural—*Z* shape and my little finger was protruding from my hand at an angle which would normally be impossible unless it was broken. My wife saw it, the women at the church saw it, and the nurse saw it.

"There is virtually no way that someone of my weight—I weigh over 260 pounds—could have fallen so awkwardly, and heavily, onto the side of a curled-up hand without sustaining some real damage. The fact that I went into shock at the scene of the accident confirmed the severity of the fall."

The first thing Graham recalls doing after he left the hospital is telephoning his pastor. "What had happened to me was simply a confirmation in our lives that Jesus is real," he avows. "He is still in the miracle business. There was no shouting or overt joy, just a simple thanks to our Father for His intervention."

Asked why he was singled out for such a miracle, Graham simply shrugs.

"God gave me a hug and a kiss when He healed my wrist and my hand," he asserts. "I don't know why I was singled out for such a miracle—I don't think I'm more worthy of receiving a miracle than anybody else. Maybe He was using me to witness on the Internet—an excellent forum for disseminating this sort of information. All

I know is that I continue to feel His presence in all aspects of my life. He continues to bless me enormously."

Graham adds that skeptics may claim that so-called miracles are nothing more than a placebo effect or, at best, a normal remission of an illness. "I can understand this attitude because it was one I once had held myself," he asserts. "However, healing a physical break cannot be faked—it cannot be likened to an illness going into unexpected remission. This was tangible, real, and unfakeable."

He further adds that the power of prayer can never be negated. "This is our communion with God. If we don't talk to Him, ask Him for assistance when we need it, thank Him for His provision in our lives, we will receive very little. This doesn't mean that God ignores us, but He is more inclined to bless us with these little extras if we submit ourselves fully to Him and try to lead a life which pleases Him."

*N*ew York City Police Officer Robert Diaz's life was careening out of control in the summer of 1989. His wife had just left him and his mother was dying from cancer. He was also having problems at work.

Robert had been troubled for a long time. As a child, his baby-sitter's daughter had sexually abused him. That led to a life where he tried to use booze and drugs to forget the assault.

As a young man, Robert would hang out on the street and in the parks all hours of the night and pay no attention when his mother asked him to please turn his life around. She would beg him to go to church. He would shout at her to mind her own business and ignore the tears in her eyes.

"I just didn't care. I blamed my mother just as much as I blamed myself for what happened to me with the baby-sitter. I was just trying to get even with the world and punish myself at the same time."

Robert thought that maybe his lifestyle would change when, in the early 1970s, he fell in love and married Gwen. But things stayed just the same—even when, twelve years later at age thirty-two, he applied and was accepted to work for the New York City Police Department.

"The job just suited me fine. I grew up in a tough Bronx neighborhood, and I knew the streets. I didn't care how dangerous things got because I didn't care about myself." Several times Robert daringly risked his life.

His heroism got him assigned to a two-and-a-half-year stint helping to guard former mayor David Dinkins, New York City's first African-American mayor. He took this job very seriously and it became a source of real pride for him.

Still, Robert continued to maintain a wild lifestyle. Eventually his behavior took a toll on his marriage. In 1989—at age thirty-five—he and his wife really hit the skids. By now, he'd been working with the police department for five years. At least three times a week he would get home close to five in the morning and then report to work just a few hours later.

Robert was always careful not to let his boozing affect his police work. He knew from talking to his buddies that a lot of cops lived the same kind of lifestyle and got away with it.

Gwen was not really someone who wanted to go to a lot of parties, and she felt increasingly isolated by her husband's behavior. Robert paid little attention. "Hey, Gwen," he told her one night. "I don't expect you to understand me. Nobody understands a cop." Then one day it all came to a head. Robert came home to find his wife gone.

Robert was grief-stricken. But more bad news was to follow. His mother was diagnosed with an incurable form of cancer and was given six to eight months to live. He was transferred to a new police detail that he didn't like. He felt lonely, isolated, and frustrated. Making matters worse, he couldn't talk to anyone because he didn't want the department to know what he was going through.

"Just what the hell are you doin'? Go get some psychological counseling," his best friend Stanley Mason, an older cop, told him.

Robert just hit the bottle harder than usual. He went on three-day drinking binges and there were times he passed out for who knew how many hours—but always in private and never on the job.

His imagination became his worst enemy. At night he would stay awake thinking about his wife and how she must be sleeping with other men. It drove him crazy.

He also agonized constantly over his mother's precarious state of health. In addition, he was now getting worried that his superiors would find out all about his private life and how he was handling his problems. Once they did, he was sure that he'd be fired—and then what?

"You don't look so well," his lieutenant told him one morning when he reported later than usual for work.

"Yeah, well, I got problems with my mom," he replied.

"Sure that's all?" his boss asked. Robert nodded. He knew that if he said anything about his personal problems, he'd never stop talking.

Tormented, Robert paced his apartment that night. His heart ached with loneliness, while his soul seemed gripped by a dark presence that he could not dispel. He felt both agitated and depressed at the same time.

As he circled his apartment like a wounded animal, Robert noticed the holstered gun lying on his couch. It seemed to beckon to him. There was no other way out. Suicide was the solution.

He lifted the .38 Smith and Wesson revolver and put the muzzle into his mouth. Robert grimaced at the bitter metallic taste of the gun. He cocked the hammer of the firearm, and everything began to move in slow motion. This was it. There wouldn't be any more painful tomorrows.

"I slowly pulled back the hammer," Robert describes, "it was as if time had suddenly slowed done and gone out of sync. I have this noisy apartment in the Bronx, and everything just went quiet. You could hear a pin drop."

Robert remembers watching his finger tighten around the trigger of his gun when all of a sudden he heard something. It was a voice in his head that he did not recognize. It was pleading with him, repeating the same word over and over again—"No, no!"

Robert remembers looking around, feeling confused. Who was talking to him in the empty apartment? It was strange, but it seemed like there was a light permeating the room. He removed the gun from his mouth and fell down on the couch, his eyes welling up with tears.

"It was the lowest point in my life. The worst moment I can ever remember. And yet it was also the greatest moment of my life. I just knew that God had spoken to me and that I had received a special miracle."

All Robert can remember about the moments afterward is falling asleep and awakening hours later. And when he did, once more he realized that he had experienced a miracle. God's voice had appeared in that silence and told him not to kill himself. And it was God's appearance at that moment that set him free.

Today, still living in New York, Robert is deeply religious. He has stopped drinking and has reunited with his wife. "God's miracle had remarkable results," he proclaims. "Jesus has filled the void in my life." Robert also speaks before groups of police officers. "If I can save just one cop from putting a bullet into his brain, I will feel that I have returned the favor of a new and lasting life that God gave to me."

As she lay in a Russian hospital operating room surrounded by doctors who struggled to get her heart beating again, Lia Tchebourkova, a former Moscow librarian, says she remembers not being on the table but, rather, floating above it.

For six minutes — moments that seemed an eternity to her — the sixty-seven-year-old heart patient found herself in a special place — another dimension that she longingly describes as being filled with pure white light and a sense of overwhelming love and peace.

Having grown up in the Communist system before emigrating to the United States in the 1980s, Lia says she was completely shocked to have a spiritual experience, because she had absolutely no connection with religion. "Religion was not permitted to be practiced in my country at that time," she says. "Miracles, God, and angels were considered fairy tales."

Lia's husband shared her skepticism. An engineer, he laughed at the idea of miracles. Neither one of them had ever set foot in a house of worship or ever prayed to any kind of higher being. "The only miracle we were aware of is that we managed to make enough money not to starve," says Lia.

Her attitude dramatically changed on May 3, 1984, when Lia, who had just recently received permission to emigrate to the United States, found herself in a Moscow hospital being prepared for open-heart surgery. Mostly she remembers lying there thinking about survival.

"Just as my dream of coming to America was about to come true, I developed heart problems," she says. "I thought, 'Probably I will die here.' I just kept having these thoughts that something was going to go wrong with the operation. We had excellent doctors, but I guess I was suffering from nerves.

"The surgeon gave me a sedative to relax me, and there I was lying on a gurney while they waited for the anesthesia to kick in. How long does that take—a few minutes? All I remember is lying there and looking at the walls." Lia realized with amazement that the walls were glowing. "That was more than fifteen years ago and I can still clearly remember it," she says. "The walls were glowing and I thought that maybe it had something to do with the medication."

Soon, despite the flurry of activity surrounding her, Lia could recall nothing but the last words of the surgeon urging her to relax. It was only after her return to wherever her soul had temporarily departed that she learned that her heart had stopped beating for nearly six minutes. Just as she had feared, something had gone wrong—or had it?

"All of a sudden," says Lia, "I was somewhere else. I was—how do you say it—completely out of my body. I was floating above it and looking down at myself and thinking, 'Oh, who cares. I don't want to have to deal with that.'"

Most interesting to her was what she describes as a beautiful blue-green white light. "It was so bright that I wanted to close my eyes—but I couldn't. I was just drawn to it. I knew at the same time that people were yelling in the operating room—that something was going on down there—but I just didn't care. I was so attracted to the light; I just wanted to follow it."

Lia floated toward the light and, for the first time in her life, she experienced a feeling of overwhelming peace and love. "If the fact that I survived the operation after my heart stopped beating was miraculous, this feeling was more so," she declares. "It was love—God's love—and I was being attended to in some way by God.

"Once in Russia my family took me out to the country and I stood on a mountaintop overlooking the Black Sea," she continues. "I'll never forget that feeling of awe I had at the time—a feeling of how much wonder there was in the world. And that's the kind of feeling I was experiencing right now. It was a big feeling that came over me—as if God was gently surrounding me and keeping me calm and safe.

"There were points of bright light along the way that almost looked human, but weren't really," Lia submits. "It's hard to explain. They looked like nothing and yet I sensed they were alive. But there was one light that was brightest of all—the leader. Maybe God—and that's the light that held all my attention. I felt the presence of the others, but this one had the most presence of all.

"I was basking in this special light. I was feeling loved, peaceful, healthy, and happy. Never had I had all those emotions all at the same time. And then something even more incredible happened. That bright light started communicating with me."

Lia describes the voice she heard as sweet and beautiful. It told her that it was not her time. She could not stay; she had to go back. "I wanted to argue," says Lia, "but before I could say anything I found myself being pulled back through a long tunnel. I tried to struggle against that. I was emotionally hurt that I couldn't stay close to that light. But I was now moving backward so fast—back to my physical body."

Lia's heart began beating again. She found herself back on the surgical table, looking up at concerned doctors who were still pounding on her chest.

"They were so desperate to bring me back here, and I was so desperate to be on the other side," she says. "But they were working so hard—yelling my name, slapping my face, pulling on my arms and legs. I think I opened my eyes and laughed."

The surgery repaired Lia completely. For a week, a score of doctors visited Lia's bedside to ask her endless questions. "They were trying to find out what had gone wrong, but they didn't want to hear me tell them that nothing had gone wrong. Things for me had gone very right."

Lia says that when she walked out of that hospital she was a different person. "Every night I was having dreams," she attests. "There were visions. There were psychic experiences that I couldn't explain. My son came over and said he had a terrible headache, so I put my hands on his head and it went away. My sister had pains in her stomach and I put my hands there and the pain went away. I was a changed person. I would touch people and they would feel better—comforted by me."

Lia says her new ability to heal puzzled her. "I didn't know exactly how I did it—I'm still confused. But when I touched someone who was sick, I could feel the pain in the body and I could direct energy to those organs that needed assistance. It didn't work every time. If God wants someone to join Him, I couldn't stop it."

Several months after her surgery, Lia's dream of coming to the United States finally came true. Although it was initially difficult for her to find work, she was determined to do something where she could help people.

For she now knew that, despite what the Communists had taught her, there was a God out there. "This was the real miracle, and the reason I think I went through this illness. It was time for me to find God—and I did."

The agency that brought Lia to America helped her find a job as a home companion, even though it didn't pay much. "The job was exactly what I was looking for—a chance to help elderly and sick people. I haven't cured anybody lately, but when I'm with a client and hold their hands, they tell me they feel special—better—and that's good enough for me."

Lia admits that many times while sitting alone in her apartment she thinks about those moments on the operating table. "Did I really die for six minutes? Did I really speak to God? Was I in a special place? Why me?" Many questions, she admits, but too few answers.

"All I know is that this experience—I call it God's miracle—changed my entire life. I'm now certain that we are more than physical beings. I'm sure that God is real. And I'm sure that miracles happen because one happened to me."

$\mathcal{S}$ally Kaye, of Evanston, Illinois, had no idea what had happened to her biological parents. All her adopted parents could tell her for certain was that she had four brothers and sisters and that they still might be living in the Chicago area. Sally knew the last names of her missing family, but nothing ever turned up on the Internet when she searched for her family name. Once she had even hired a private detective with no success.

It was a cold night in 1995, and Sally was a little depressed. She loved her adopted parents, but she just wanted to know what had happened to her original parents and siblings. She lay in bed praying—something she had not done for a while: "Please God, let me not die without knowing more about the mother who gave birth to me." The house she was now living in was located just off the shores of Lake Michigan, and Sally could hear waves pounding off the rocks not too far away.

Out of the noise and darkness came a voice that night: "Don't give up; don't give up," the voice urged her. The next night, the same thing happened.

Sally didn't know what to make of it.

"I didn't know if it was God, an angel, or my writer's imagination. But I knew it wasn't my imagination that made me feel I needed to go to church on Sunday."

Sally was not religious. Raised a Christian Scientist, she had shied away from her faith at an early age. But now the urge to go to church was overwhelming.

As Sally walked into the church, she looked at the faces of the worshipers. Maybe she would see someone who looked like her—some kind of family resemblance.

Finally she spotted a young man whose face reminded her of her own. She walked up to him and said, "Hey, do you know me?"

"I sure wasn't shy about it," Sally says now.

The young man stared at Sally blankly. He had no memory of her whatsoever. Still, Sally had the feeling that this person looked familiar. So she went back to that church the next Sunday and saw him again. She asked to meet his mother.

When Sally visited the young man's house, she felt as if she were getting warmer. She gave the woman her birth family's last name and everything she knew about them, and the young man's mother turned out to be one of Sally's birthmother's cousins, who had an idea of where Sally's birthmother was living.

Going to church that day turned out to be crucial. Within eight years Sally had located her biological parents, all four of her missing brothers and sisters, and both of her grandmothers. It was an incredible task since they were scattered throughout the United States. In that time, she heard the mysterious voice two more times on two different nights.

"It was one of the greatest miracles of my life to be adopted and still see all of my family. I continue to stay in touch with all of them. Even though I was adopted and well taken care of, I wanted to know everything about my past and now I do. To me, that's the most miraculous thing in the world."

Before she found her biological family, Sally recalls that she always felt somewhat depressed. That no longer is true. "I don't walk around feeling like a piece of me is missing, and I thank God for helping me."

epression had taken a desperate toll on twenty-one-year-old Kelly Lynch of Canton, Ohio, and she thought that the only escape from her everyday nightmare would be suicide. It was a cool morning on October 8, 1987, when she took her father's gun, placed it against her chest, and slowly pulled the trigger.

Kelly's life seemed to fall apart in the previous year. Health problems had necessitated a hysterectomy, destroying her dream of having children someday. She and her husband had separated. And her aunt had committed suicide.

Kelly was living with her parents. She waited for her father to leave for work, and then she went to the den and found his Derringer.

Her father told her later that he'd had a gut-wrenching feeling that he should hide that gun somewhere else that morning. But he didn't, and Kelly knew just where to find it.

Kelly took some sedatives first, walked back into her room, and calmly sat down upon her bed. She wrote a simple suicide note to her parents, telling them she was sorry, that she loved them, and to say goodbye to her brothers for her. Then she lay back on the bed.

Kelly thought carefully about where she should shoot herself.

She feared that if she shot herself in the head, she might live and become a vegetable for the rest of her life. She didn't want to be a burden. She had already been in and out of the hospital for her emotional state, and she didn't want her family to have to worry about her anymore. So she put the gun to her heart.

But first she called two people. Her youth pastor at church wasn't in. Her estranged husband was too busy at work to talk. So she put down the phone, put the gun to her chest, pulled the trigger, and fired.

Kelly cannot remember exactly how long she lay in bed bleeding. But soon she heard a voice telling her to get help. She believes it was God. A feeling swept over her: She wanted to live. "I don't really know how to explain this voice," she says. "I knew it was Him and He was encouraging me not to die. I was in shock and everything else, but at the same time now this feeling of peace began to surround me. I just knew then that I was going to be okay."

Despite her wound, Kelly called her mother at work and told her what she had done. Kelly's mother screamed, and dropped the phone. It was Kelly who called 911, and an ambulance came just after Kelly's mom arrived. "Amazingly, there I was walking around the house with a bullet in me," Kelly recalls. "When my mother saw the blood on my chest I think she went into shock."

The paramedics removed the bullet from Kelly's back in the ambulance. X-rays were taken as soon as she came into the hospital.

The surgeon entered her room looking astonished. He showed her the x-ray, and pointed. He said to Kelly, "Young lady, you missed your heart by a quarter of an inch. You had a God-guided bullet." The bullet hadn't hit a single vital organ.

Kelly's recovery was swift and easy. Her life was transformed.

Kelly has become a happy person. She has stopped

taking antidepressants because she is more grateful for and happier with her life than ever before. "This life-changing episode was also a miracle in that it so affected my life and gave me a new direction," she declares. Today she testifies to youth groups about her experience, hoping to help young people who are suicidal or depressed. "My walk with the Lord is a lot stronger and a lot deeper these days. I know that God has a plan for my life and that He is in control."

Kelly says she is always reminded of that because the bullet wound left a scar in the sign of a small cross on her chest. When Kelly saw it for the first time, she heard God's voice one more time. "He said, 'Every time you look at that scar and see the cross, I want you to remember how much I love you.'"